TRUE DEVOTION
TO MARY

"The more we honor the Blessed Virgin, the more we honor Jesus Christ, because we honor Mary only that we may the more perfectly honor Jesus, since we go to her only as the way by which we are to find the end we are seeking, which is Jesus."

—St. Louis De Montfort

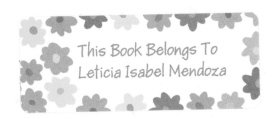

This Book Belongs To
Leticia Isabel Mendoza

D0954254

St. Louis-Marie Grignion De Montfort
1673-1716
Statue in St. Peter's Basilica, Rome

TRUE DEVOTION TO MARY

By
ST. LOUIS-MARIE GRIGNION DE MONTFORT

Translated from the Original French by
Father Frederick William Faber, D.D.
Priest of the Oratory

Edited and Annotated by
The Fathers of the Company of Mary

> *Jesus Christ is not known as He ought to be because Mary has been up to this time unknown.*
>   —St. Louis De Montfort

TAN BOOKS AND PUBLISHERS, INC.
Rockford, Illinois 61105

Imprimi Potest: A. Josselin, S.M.M.
                  Superior General

Nihil Obstat: John M. A. Fearns, S.T.D.
                  Censor Librorum

Imprimatur: ✝ Francis Cardinal Spellman, D.D.
                  Archbishop of New York
                  September 26, 1949

Copyright © 1941 by the Fathers of the Company of Mary.

Library of Congress Catalog Card No.: 85-50571

ISBN: 0-89555-279-5

The typography of this book is the property of TAN Books and Publishers, Inc., and may not be reproduced, in whole or in part, without written permission of the publisher.

Printed and bound in the United States of America.

TAN BOOKS AND PUBLISHERS, INC.
P.O. Box 424
Rockford, Illinois 61105

1985

FROM THE POPES

Pope Pius IX declared that St. Louis De Montfort's devotion to Mary was the best and most acceptable form of devotion to Our Lady.

Pope Leo XIII granted a plenary indulgence to those who make St. Louis De Montfort's act of consecration to the Blessed Virgin. On his deathbed he renewed the act himself and invoked the heavenly aid of St. Louis De Montfort, whom he had beatified in 1888.

Pope St. Pius X: "I heartily recommend *True Devotion to The Blessed Virgin,* so admirably written by Blessed De Montfort, and to all who read it grant the Apostolic Benediction."

Pope Benedict XV: "A book of high authority and unction."

Pope Pius XI: "I have practiced this devotion ever since my youth."

Pope Pius XII: "The greatest force behind all his [St. Louis De Montfort's] apostolic ministry and his great secret for attracting and winning souls for Jesus was his devotion to Mary." (*From Canonization address, July 20, 1947*).

Pope Paul VI: "We are convinced without any doubt that devotion to Our Lady is essentially joined with devotion to Christ, that it assures a firmness of conviction to faith in Him and in His Church, a vital adherence to Him and to His Church which, without devotion to Mary, would be impoverished and compromised."

Pope John Paul II: "The reading of this book was a decisive turning-point in my life. I say 'turning-point,' but in fact it was a long inner journey. . . . This 'perfect devotion' is indispensable to anyone who means to give himself without reserve to Christ and to the work of redemption." "It is from Montfort that I have taken my motto: *'Totus tuus'* ('I am all thine'). Someday I'll have to tell you Montfortians how I discovered De Montfort's *Treatise on True Devotion to Mary,* and how often I had to reread it to understand it."

Vatican Council II: "The maternal duty of Mary toward men in no way obscures or diminishes this unique mediation of Christ, but rather shows its power. All her saving influence on men originates not from some inner necessity, but from the divine pleasure. It flows forth from the superabundance of the merits of Christ, rests on His mediation, depends entirely on it and draws all its power from it." ". . . the practices and exercises of devotion to her recommended by the Church in the course of the centuries [are to] be treasured. . . ." (*Lumen Gentium:* 60, 67).

CONTENTS

— Part One —

Devotion
to the Blessed Virgin Mary

— Part Two —

Perfect Devotion
to the Blessed Virgin Mary
or
Perfect Consecration to Jesus Christ

— Supplement —

ABOUT ST. LOUIS DE MONTFORT

St. Louis Marie Grignion de la Bacheleraie, who abandoned his family name for that of his birthplace, was born on January 31, 1673 in the little town of Montfort-la-Canne, which is located in Brittany, France. He studied for the priesthood at St. Sulpice in Paris, having made the 200-mile journey there on foot. He was ordained a priest in 1700, at the age of 27.

St. Louis De Montfort had wanted to become a missionary in Canada, but he was advised to remain in France. There he traveled around the western part of the country, from diocese to diocese and from parish to parish, instructing the people, preaching, helping the poor, hearing confessions, giving retreats, opening schools and rebuilding church buildings. His labors were almost miraculously fruitful. He stated that never did a sinner resist after being touched by him with a Rosary.

But because he encountered great opposition from religious authorities—in particular, being forbidden by the Bishop of Poitiers to preach in his diocese—he decided to travel to Rome to ask the Holy Father if he was doing God's Will and whether he should continue as before. St. Louis De Montfort walked to Rome—a thousand miles—and put his case to Pope Clement XI. The Pope told him to continue his traveling missionary work, and named him Missionary Apostolic, but told him always to be sure to work under obedience to the diocesan authorities.

One of St. Louis De Montfort's greatest problems was the opposition he encountered from propagators of the Jansenist heresy, which was then very active in France. The Jansenists spread an atmosphere of harshness and moral rigorism, claiming that human nature was radically corrupted by Original Sin (as opposed to the Catholic teaching that human nature is still essentially good, though fallen, and although it has suffered a darkening of the intellect and weakening of the will). The Jansenists denied that God's mercy is available to all, and they allowed only infrequent reception of the Sacraments of Penance and the Holy Eucharist, and only after long and severe preparation—with Holy Communion being looked upon as a reward rather than a remedy. Also, they taught that God should always be addressed with fear and trembling. These tenets resembled those of Calvinism. Although Jansenism had been condemned by the Church twice even before St. Louis De Montfort's birth, its teachings continued to spread and to influence people for a century. In contrast, St. Louis De Montfort preached confidence in Mary and union with her Divine Son.

St. Louis De Montfort founded two religious orders: the Daughters of Wisdom, begun in 1703 from a number of poor and afflicted girls at the Hospital of Poitiers, where he was temporary chaplain, and the Missionaries of the Company of Mary (Montfort Fathers and Brothers), founded in 1715. The Brothers of St. Gabriel, a teaching order, also claim St. Louis De Montfort as their spiritual father.

St. Louis De Montfort left several writings, the most famous being *The Secret of the Rosary, True Devotion to Mary,* and *The Secret of Mary.* These books were based on sermons he had given when traveling around France. By spreading devotion to the Blessed Virgin Mary, St. Louis De Montfort was teaching souls to love the devil's great enemy. (In *True Devotion to Mary,* he states that the devil fears Mary more than all angels and men, and in a sense more than God Himself—see no. 52). At the saint's beatification investigation, many witnesses testified that during his life they had heard struggles between him and the devil, including the sound of fist blows and the swish of whips.

St. Louis De Montfort exhausted his great physical strength by his apostolic labors. On his deathbed in Saint-Laurent-sur-Sèvre, at age 43, he kissed the crucifix and a statue of the Blessed Mother. Apparently speaking to the devil, he exclaimed: "In vain do you attack me; I am between Jesus and Mary! I have finished my course: All is over. I shall sin no more!" Then he died peacefully on April 28, 1716. His feast day is April 28, the day of his birth in Heaven. St. Louis De Montfort's writings were examined by the Holy See, which pronounced that there was nothing in them to hinder his beatification and canonization. He was canonized a saint in 1947.

ABOUT *TRUE DEVOTION TO MARY*

St. Louis De Montfort himself prophesied regarding *True Devotion to Mary:* "I clearly foresee that raging beasts shall come in fury to tear with their diabolical teeth this little writing and him whom the Holy Ghost has made use of to write it—or at least to smother it in the darkness and silence of a coffer, that it may not appear. They shall even attack and persecute those who shall read it and carry it out in practice." (T.D., no. 114). This prediction was fulfilled to the letter. Throughout the whole 18th century, the spiritual sons of St. Louis De Montfort were persecuted by the Jansenists for their zeal in spreading this devotion; the precious manuscript of De Montfort remained hidden during the troubled times of the French Revolution and was brought to light only in the year 1842, when it was found in a chest of old books by a Montfort Father.

The title page from *True Devotion* was missing, and the book has been variously known as *True Devotion to the Blessed Virgin, Treatise on True Devotion to Mary,* and *True Devotion to Mary*—the phrase "true devotion" being drawn from chapter III of Part 1, wherein St. Louis De Montfort distinguishes between true devotion and false devotion to Mary. Over the years, however, the phrase "true devotion" has come to be used in reference to the *Perfect* Devotion to Mary which is expounded on in Part 2 of the book.

St. Louis De Montfort was the one to whom it was given to explain thoroughly the path "to Jesus through Mary" and to shape it into a definite method of spiritual life. He does not propose some special or "extra" prayers, but rather, a devotion which essentially consists of one single act which, under various forms and conditions, we apply to our whole life, both interior and exterior. This devotion leads to a permanent disposition of living and acting habitually in dependence on Mary; it embraces one's entire life, not just one's prayer times or specifically religious acts.

St. Louis De Montfort knew that Mary is the pathway to her Son, leading souls quickly and securely to Jesus Christ, the Eternal Wisdom.

Inflamed with holy love St. Louis De Montfort wrote many poems to the Divine Wisdom, including the following fervent lines:

Divine Wisdom, I love Thee unto folly.
I am Thy lover.
Thou alone in this world I seek,
Thou alone I desire.
I am a man gone mad with love,
Forever chasing Thee.

Tell me who Thou art,
For I am half blind.
I can discern only
That Thou art a secret I must fathom.
Show Thyself fully to my soul
Which dies for love of Thee.

Where dost Thou live,
Wisdom Divine?
Must I cross continents or seas
To find Thee,

Or fly across the skies?
I am ready to go wherever Thou art,
Not counting the costs, to possess Thee.

To Jesus through Mary: This is the sublime secret of holiness set forth by St. Louis De Montfort in *True Devotion to Mary*—a book which ranks among the greatest spiritual masterpieces ever penned, a book which seems to have been inspired by the Holy Ghost Himself. May this book lead many souls to a deep and faithful love of Our Lord Jesus Christ.

PREFACE
by
Cardinal O'Connell

The doctrine of Blessed Louis Marie Grignion De Montfort needs neither introduction nor explanation to those who are conversant with the spiritual life. It is well known that the practice of the Perfect Devotion to the Blessed Virgin which he taught is widespread among priests, religious and even lay people throughout the world. It is gratifying to note that its beneficial influence is felt in many sections of our own country.

This widespread propagation of the Perfect Devotion in many respects resembles the growth of the mustard seed spoken of in the Gospel: It had a humble beginning, grew without great exterior display, and, by the grace of the Holy Ghost, spread throughout the entire Church. This new edition of the manual will contribute toward making it still better known. It is my happy privilege to recommend it to everyone, following therein the example of our late Holy Father of blessed memory, Pius X.

I have known this form of devotion for many years and I have never hesitated to recommend it to those in whom the grace of God seemed to be at work, drawing them toward a deeper and more intense spiritual life. As Rector of the American College in Rome, I proposed and taught it to the seminarians as an excellent means of acquiring the holiness of their priestly ideal. It was with my encouragement that

there was formed among them a "Blessed De
Montfort Society." The Legion of Mary, which we
have heartily encouraged in our diocese with such
happy results, derives from the spiritual teachings of
Montfort to such an extent that he is said to be the
"tutor of the Legion" (Handbook, p. 51). Several confraternities of Mary, Queen of All Hearts, are at present propagating the Perfect Devotion in various centers throughout the United States.

The more we reflect, the more we realize that the
mission of Christianity is to take possession of man
in his entirety in order to transform him into a soul
worthy of Heaven. Hence, Pius XI, in speaking of
Christian Education, says that its "proper and immediate end is to cooperate with divine grace in forming the true and perfect Christian, that is, to form
Christ Himself in those regenerated by Baptism." In
this work of transformation, a definite part has been
assigned by God to the Blessed Virgin Mary, that of
leading souls to Jesus Christ, and of keeping them in
His love.

Hence, the role of Mary, Mother of God and
Mediatrix of All Grace, ought not to be overlooked.
Indeed, the recognition of the high dignity granted her
by God leads her clients toward a richer understanding of the mysteries of Christ and a fuller participation in the fruits of the Redemption.

Our Holy Mother the Church has recognized the
merit of the *Treatise on the True Devotion to Mary* in
conferring upon its author the honor of beatification.
She has approved and enriched with numerous indulgences the Confraternity of Mary, Queen of All
Hearts. It is our conviction that a wider diffusion of
this work "of great unction and authority"—to use the

words of His Holiness, Benedict XV—will draw souls from every walk of life to a greater interior perfection and a fuller development of Christian piety.

W. Card. O'Connell,

Abp. Boston

December 8, 1940

FATHER FABER'S PREFACE

It was in the year 1846 or 1847, at St. Wilfrid's, that I first studied the life and spirit of the Venerable Grignion De Montfort; and now, after more than fifteen years, it may be allowable to say that those who take him for their master will hardly be able to name a saint or ascetical writer to whose grace and spirit their mind will be more subject than to his. We may not yet call him saint; but the process of his beatification is so far and so favorably advanced that we may not have long to wait before he will be raised upon the altars of the Church.

There are few men in the eighteenth century who have more strongly upon them the marks of the man of Providence than this Elias-like missionary of the Holy Ghost and of Mary. His entire life was such an exhibition of the holy folly of the Cross that his biographers unite in always classing him with St. Simon Salo and St. Philip Neri. Clement XI made him a missionary apostolic in France, in order that he might spend his life in fighting against Jansenism, so far as it affected the salvation of souls. Since the Apostolical Epistles it would be hard to find words that burn so marvelously as the twelve pages of his prayer for the Missionaries of the Holy Ghost, to which I earnestly refer all those who find it hard to keep up under their numberless trials the first fires of the love of souls.

He was at once persecuted and venerated everywhere. His amount of work, like that of St. Anthony

of Padua, is incredible, and indeed, inexplicable. He
wrote some spiritual treatises which have already had
a remarkable influence on the Church during the few
years they have been known, and bid fair to have a
much wider influence in years to come. His preaching, his writing and his conversation were all impreg-
nated with prophecy and with anticipations of the
later ages of the Church. He comes forward like
another St. Vincent Ferrer, as if on the days bordering
on the Last Judgment, and proclaims that he brings an
authentic message from God about the greater honor
and wider knowledge and more prominent love of His
Blessed Mother, and her connection with the second
advent of her Son. He founded two religious congregations—one of men and one of women—which
have been quite extraordinarily successful; and yet he
died at the age of forty-three in 1716, after only six-
teen years of priesthood.

It was on the 12th of May, 1853, that the decree
was pronounced at Rome declaring his writing to be
exempt from all error which could be a bar to his
canonization. In this very treatise on the veritable
devotion to our Blessed Lady, he has recorded this
prophecy: "I clearly foresee that raging brutes will
come in fury to tear with their diabolical teeth this little writing and him whom the Holy Ghost has made
use of to write it; or at least to envelop it in the silence
of a coffer, in order that it may not appear."
Nevertheless, he prophesies both its appearance and
its success. All this was fulfilled to the letter. The
author died in 1716, and the treatise was found by ac-
cident by one of the priests of his congregation of St.
Laurent-sur-Sèvre in 1842. The existing superior was
able to attest the handwriting as being that of the

venerable founder, and the autograph was sent to Rome to be examined in the process of canonization.

All those who are likely to read this book love God, and lament that they do not love Him more; all desire something for His glory—the spread of some good work, the success of some devotion, the coming of some good time. One man has been striving for years to overcome a particular fault, and has not succeeded. Another mourns, and almost wonders while he mourns, that so few of his relations and friends have been converted to the Faith. One grieves that he has not devotion enough; another that he has a cross to carry which is a peculiarly impossible cross to him; while a third has domestic troubles and family unhappinesses which feel almost incompatible with his salvation; and for all these things prayer appears to bring so little remedy.

But what is the remedy that is wanted? What is the remedy indicated by God Himself? If we may rely on the disclosures of the saints, it is an immense increase of devotion to our Blessed Lady; but, remember, nothing short of an immense one. Here in England, Mary is not half enough preached. Devotion to her is low and thin and poor. It is frightened out of its wits by the sneers of heresy. It is always invoking human respect and carnal prudence, wishing to make Mary so little of a Mary that Protestants may feel at ease about her. Its ignorance of theology makes it unsubstantial and unworthy. It is not the prominent characteristic of our religion which it ought to be. It has no faith in itself. Hence it is that Jesus is not loved, that heretics are not converted, that the Church is not exalted; that souls which might be saints wither and dwindle; that the Sacraments are not rightly frequented, or souls enthusiastically evangelized.

Jesus is obscured because Mary is kept in the background. Thousands of souls perish because Mary is withheld from them. It is the miserable, unworthy shadow which we call our devotion to the Blessed Virgin that is the cause of all these wants and blights, these evils and omissions and declines. Yet, if we are to believe the revelations of the saints, God is pressing for a greater, a wider, a stronger, quite another devotion to His Blessed Mother. I cannot think of a higher work or a broader vocation for anyone than the simple spreading of this peculiar devotion of the Venerable Grignion De Montfort. Let a man but try it for himself, and his surprise at the graces it brings with it, and the transformations it causes in his soul, will soon convince him of its otherwise almost incredible efficacy as a means for the salvation of men, and for the coming of the kingdom of Christ. Oh, if Mary were but known, there would be no coldness to Jesus then! Oh, if Mary were but known, how much more wonderful would be our faith, and how different would our Communions be! Oh, if Mary were but known, how much happier, how much holier, how much less worldly should we be, and how much more should we be living images of our sole Lord and Saviour, her dearest and most blessed Son!

I have translated the whole treatise myself, and have taken great pains with it, and have been scrupulously faithful. At the same time, I would venture to warn the reader that one perusal will be very far from making him master of it. If I may dare to say so, there is a growing feeling of something inspired and supernatural about it, as we go on studying it; and with that we cannot help experiencing, after repeated readings of it, that its novelty never seems to wear off, nor its fullness to be diminished, nor the fresh fragrance and sensible fire of its unction ever to abate. May the Holy Ghost, the Divine Zealot of Jesus and Mary, deign to give a new blessing to this work in England; and may He please to console us quickly with the canonization of this new apostle and fiery missionary of His most dear and most Immaculate spouse, and still more with the speedy coming of that great age of the Church which is to be the Age of Mary!

> F. W. Faber
> Priest of the Oratory
> Presentation of Our Blessed Lady
> November 21, 1862

TRUE DEVOTION
TO MARY

The more the Holy Ghost finds Mary, His dear and inseparable spouse, in any soul, the more active and mighty He becomes in producing Jesus Christ in that soul, and that soul in Jesus Christ.
—St. Louis De Montfort

St. Louis De Montfort at the feet of Mary,
Queen of All Hearts,
in Queen of All Hearts Chapel, Rome.

PRELIMINARY REMARKS
by St. Louis De Montfort

1. It was through the most holy Virgin Mary that Jesus came into the world, and it is also through her that He has to reign in the world.

2. Mary was singularly hidden during her life. It is on this account that the Holy Ghost and the Church call her *Alma Mater*—"Mother secret and hidden."[1] Her humility was so profound that she had no inclination on earth more powerful or more constant than that of hiding herself, from herself as well as from every other creature, so as to be known to God only.

3. He heard her prayers when she begged to be hidden, to be humbled and to be treated as in all respects poor and of no account. He took pleasure in hiding her from all human creatures, in her conception, in her birth, in her life, in her mysteries, and in her resurrection and Assumption. Even her parents did not know her, and the angels often asked one another: "Who is that?" (*Cant.* 3:6; 8:5) because the Most High either had hidden her from them, or if He did reveal anything, it was nothing compared to what He kept undisclosed.

4. God the Father consented that she should work no miracle, at least no public one, during her life, although He had given her the power to do so. God the Son consented that she should hardly ever speak, though He had communicated His wisdom to her. God the Holy Ghost, though she was His faithful spouse, consented that His Apostles and Evangelists

3

should speak very little of her, and no more than was necessary to make Jesus Christ known.

5. Mary is the excellent masterpiece of the Most High, the knowledge and possession of which He has reserved to Himself. Mary is the admirable Mother of the Son, who took pleasure in humbling and concealing her during her life in order to favor her humility, calling her by the name of "woman" (*Jn.* 2:4; 19:26), as if she were a stranger, although in His heart He esteemed and loved her above all angels and all men. Mary is the "sealed fountain" (*Cant.* 4:12), the faithful spouse of the Holy Ghost, to whom He alone has entrance. Mary is the sanctuary and the repose of the Holy Trinity, where God dwells more magnificently and more divinely than in any other place in the universe, not excepting His dwelling between the Cherubim and Seraphim. Nor is any creature, no matter how pure, allowed to enter into that sanctuary except by a great and special privilege.

6. I say with the saints, the divine[2] Mary is the terrestrial paradise of the New Adam, where He was made flesh by the operation of the Holy Ghost, in order to work there incomprehensible marvels. She is the grand and divine world of God, where there are beauties and treasures unspeakable. She is the magnificence of the Most High, where He hid, as in her bosom, His only Son, and in Him all that is most excellent and most precious. Oh, what grand and hidden things that mighty God has wrought in this admirable creature, as she herself had to acknowledge, in spite of her profound humility: "He that is mighty hath done great things to me." (*Lk.* 1:49). The world knows them not, because it is both incapable and unworthy of such knowledge.

7. The saints have said admirable things of this holy city of God; and, as they themselves avow, they were never more eloquent and more content than when they spoke of her. Yet, after all they have said, they cry out that the height of her merits, which she has raised up to the throne of the Divinity, cannot be fully seen; that the breadth of her charity, which is broader than the earth, is in truth immeasurable; that the length of her power, which she exercises even over God Himself, is incomprehensible; and finally, that the depth of her humility, and of all her virtues and graces, is an abyss which never can be sounded. O height incomprehensible! O breadth unspeakable! O length immeasurable! O abyss impenetrable!

8. Every day, from one end of the earth to the other, in the highest heights of the heavens and in the profoundest depths of the abysses, everything preaches, everything publishes, the admirable Mary! The nine choirs of angels, men of all ages, sexes, conditions and religions, the good and the bad, nay, even the devils themselves, willingly or unwillingly, are compelled by the force of truth to call her "Blessed." St. Bonaventure tells us that all the angels in Heaven cry out incessantly to her: "Holy, holy, holy Mary, Mother of God and Virgin";[3] and that they offer to her, millions and millions of times a day, the Angelical Salutation, *Ave Maria,* prostrating themselves before her, and begging of her in her graciousness to honor them with some of her commands. Even St. Michael, as St. Augustine says, although the prince of the heavenly court, is the most zealous in honoring her and causing her to be honored, and is always anxiously awaiting the honor of going at her bidding to render service to some one of her servants.[4]

9. The whole earth is full of her glory, especially among Christians, by whom she is taken as the protectress of many kingdoms, provinces, dioceses and cities. Many cathedrals are consecrated to God under her name. There is not a church without an altar in her honor, not a country nor a canton where there are not some miraculous images where all sorts of evils are cured and all sorts of good gifts obtained. Who can count the confraternities and congregations in her honor? How many religious orders have been founded in her name and under her protection? How many members in these confraternities, and how many religious men and women in all these orders, who publish her praises and confess her mercies! There is not a little child who, as it lisps the Hail Mary, does not praise her. There is scarcely a sinner who, even in his obduracy, has not some spark of confidence in her. Nay, the very devils in Hell respect her while they fear her.

10. After that, we must cry out with the saints: *"De Maria numquam satis"*—"Of Mary there is never enough." We have not yet praised, exalted, honored, loved and served Mary as we ought. She deserves still more praise, still more respect, still more love, and still more service.

11. After that, we must say with the Holy Ghost: "All the glory of the King's daughter is within." (*Ps.* 44:14). The outward glory which Heaven and earth rival each other in laying at her feet is as nothing in comparison with that which she receives within from the Creator and which is not known by creatures, who in their littleness are unable to penetrate the secret of secrets of the King.

12. After that, we must cry out with the Apostle,

"Eye has not seen, nor ear heard, nor man's heart comprehend" (*1 Cor.* 2:9) the beauties, the grandeurs, the excellences of Mary—the miracle of the miracles[5] of grace, of nature and of glory. "If you wish to comprehend the Mother," says a saint,[6] "comprehend the Son; for she is the worthy Mother of God." "Here let every tongue be mute."

13. It is with a particular joy that my heart has dictated what I have just written, in order to show that the divine Mary has been up to this time unknown,[7] and that this is one of the reasons that Jesus Christ is not known as He ought to be. If then, as is certain, the knowledge and the kingdom of Jesus Christ are to come into the world, they will be but a necessary consequence of the knowledge and the kingdom of the most holy Virgin Mary, who brought Him into the world for the first time, and will make His second advent full of splendor.

NOTES

1. Antiphon to the Blessed Virgin for Advent; also the hymn, *Ave Maris Stella.*
2. ". . . the word 'divine' may be used without attributing the nature of divinity to the person or thing thus qualified. We speak of our own prayers, whether addressed to God or to His saints, as a 'divine service.' The Psalmist speaks of us all as being gods and sons of the Most High; and yet no one takes offense, because the sense given to the words uttered is understood. Mary may be called 'divine' because divinely chosen for the divine office of Mother" of a divine Person, Jesus Christ. (Cardinal Vaughan, Preface to the English edition of *True Devotion*).
3. St. Bonaventure, *Psalt. majus B.V., Hymn. instar Ambrosiani.*
4. Quoted by St. Bonaventure, *Speculum B.V.*, lect. III, no. 5.
5. St. John Damascene, *Oratio Ia de Nativ. B.V.*
6. St. Eucherius.
7. Meaning insufficiently known, as the immediate context shows: "Jesus Christ is not known as He ought to be."

— Part One —

DEVOTION TO THE BLESSED VIRGIN MARY

Necessity

Fundamental Truths

Choice of True Devotion to the Blessed Virgin

Chapter I

NECESSITY OF THE BLESSED VIRGIN AND OF DEVOTION TO HER

14. I avow, with all the Church, that Mary, being a mere creature that has come from the hands of the Most High, is in comparison with His Infinite Majesty less than an atom; or rather, she is nothing at all, because only He is "He who is" (*Exod.* 3:14); consequently that grand Lord, always independent and sufficient to Himself, never had, and has not now, any absolute need of the holy Virgin for the accomplishment of His will and for the manifestation of His glory. He has but to will in order to do everything.

15. Nevertheless, I say that, things being as they are now—that is, God having willed to commence and to complete His greatest works by the most holy Virgin ever since He created her—we may well think He will not change His conduct in the eternal ages; for He is God, and He changes not, either in His sentiments or in His conduct.

— Article One —
MARY WAS NECESSARY TO GOD
IN THE INCARNATION OF THE WORD

16. It was only through Mary that God the Father gave His Only-begotten to the world. Whatever sighs the patriarchs may have sent forth, whatever prayers the prophets and the saints of the Old Law may have

offered up to obtain this treasure for full four thousand years, it was only Mary who merited it and found
grace before God (*Lk.* 1:30) by the force of her
prayers and the eminence of her virtues. The world
was unworthy, says St. Augustine, to receive the Son
of God directly from the Father's hands. He gave Him
to Mary in order that the world might receive Him
through her.

The Son of God became man for our salvation; but
it was in Mary and by Mary. God the Holy Ghost
formed Jesus Christ in Mary; but it was only after
having asked her consent by one of the first ministers
of His court.

17. God the Father communicated to Mary His
fruitfulness, inasmuch as a mere creature was capable
of it, in order that He might give her the power to
produce His Son and all the members of His Mystical
Body.

18. God the Son descended into her virginal womb
as the New Adam into His terrestrial paradise, to take
His pleasure there, and to work in secret marvels of
grace.

God made Man found His liberty in seeing Himself
imprisoned in her womb. He made His omnipotence
shine forth in letting Himself be carried by that humble maiden. He found His glory and His Father's in
hiding His splendors from all creatures here below,
and revealing them to Mary only. He glorified His in-
dependence and His majesty in depending on that
sweet Virgin in His conception, in His birth, in His
presentation in the temple, in His hidden life of thirty
years, and even in His death, where she was to be
present in order that He might make with her but one
same sacrifice and be immolated to the Eternal Father

by her consent, just as Isaac of old was offered by Abraham's consent to the will of God. It is she who nourished Him, supported Him, brought Him up and then sacrificed Him for us.

Oh, admirable and incomprehensible dependence of God, which the Holy Ghost could not pass over in silence in the Gospel, although He has hidden from us nearly all the admirable things which the Incarnate Wisdom did in His hidden life—as if He would enable us, by His revelation of that at least, to understand something of its excellence and infinite glory! Jesus Christ gave more glory to God the Father by submission to His Mother during those thirty years than He would have given Him in converting the whole world by the working of the most stupendous miracles. Oh, how highly we glorify God when, to please Him, we submit ourselves to Mary, after the example of Jesus Christ, our sole Exemplar!

19. If we examine closely the rest of our Blessed Lord's life, we shall see that it was His will to begin His miracles by Mary. He sanctified St. John in the womb of his mother, St. Elizabeth, but it was by Mary's word. No sooner had she spoken than John was sanctified; and this was His first miracle of grace.

At the marriage of Cana He changed the water into wine, but it was at Mary's humble prayer; and this was His first miracle of nature. He began and continued His miracles by Mary, and He will continue them to the end of ages by Mary.

20. God the Holy Ghost, being barren in God— that is to say, not producing another Divine Person— is become fruitful by Mary, whom He has espoused. It was with her, in her, and of her that He produced His Masterpiece, which is God made Man, and that He

goes on producing daily, to the end of the world, the predestinate and the members of the Body of that adorable Head. This is the reason why He, the Holy Ghost, the more He finds Mary, His dear and inseparable spouse,[1] in any soul, the more active and mighty He becomes in producing Jesus Christ in that soul, and that soul in Jesus Christ.

21. It is not that we mean that our Blessed Lady gives the Holy Ghost His fruitfulness, as if He had it not Himself. For inasmuch as He is God, He has the same fruitfulness or capacity of producing as the Father and the Son; only He does not bring it into action, as He does not produce another Divine Person. But what we mean is that the Holy Ghost chose to make use of our Blessed Lady, though He had no absolute need of her, to bring His fruitfulness into action, by producing in her and by her Jesus Christ and His members—a mystery of grace unknown to even the wisest and most spiritual among Christians.

— Article Two —
MARY IS NECESSARY TO GOD
IN THE SANCTIFICATION OF SOULS

22. The conduct which the Three Persons of the Most Holy Trinity have deigned to pursue in the Incarnation and the first coming of Jesus Christ, They still pursue daily, in an invisible manner, throughout the whole Church; and They will still pursue it even to the consummation of ages in the last coming of Jesus Christ.

23. God the Father made an assemblage of all the waters and He named it the sea *(mare)*. He made an assemblage of all His graces and he called it Mary

(Maria).[2] This great God has a most rich treasury in which He has laid up all that He has of beauty and splendor, of rarity and preciousness, including even His own Son: and this immense treasury is none other than Mary, whom the saints have named the Treasure of the Lord,[3] out of whose plenitude all men are made rich.

24. God the Son has communicated to His Mother all that He acquired by His life and His death, His infinite merits and His admirable virtues; and He has made her the treasurer of all that His Father gave Him for His inheritance. It is by her that He applies His merits to His members, and that He communicates His virtues, and distributes His graces. She is His mysterious canal; she is His aqueduct, through which He makes His mercies flow gently and abundantly.

25. To Mary, His faithful spouse, God the Holy Ghost has communicated His unspeakable gifts; and He has chosen her to be the dispenser of all He possesses, in such wise that she distributes to whom she wills, as much as she wills, as she wills and when she wills, all His gifts and graces. The Holy Ghost gives no heavenly gift to men which He does not have pass through her virginal hands. Such has been the will of God, who has willed that we should have everything through Mary; so that she who, impoverished, humbled, and who hid herself even unto the abyss of nothingness by her profound humility her whole life long, should now be enriched and exalted and honored by the Most High. Such are the sentiments of the Church and the holy Fathers.[4]

26. If I were speaking to the freethinkers of these times, I would prove what I have said so simply here,

drawing it out more at length, and confirming it by the Holy Scriptures and the Fathers, quoting the original passages, and adducing various solid reasons, which may be seen at length in the book of Father Poiré, *La Triple Couronne de la Ste. Vierge.* But as I speak particularly to the poor and simple, who being of good will, and having more faith than the common run of scholars, believe more simply and more meritoriously, I content myself with stating the truth quite plainly, without stopping to quote the Latin passages, which they would not understand. Nevertheless, without making much research, I shall not fail to bring forward some of them from time to time. But now let us go on with our subject.

27. Inasmuch as grace perfects nature, and glory perfects grace, it is certain that Our Lord is still, in Heaven, as much the Son of Mary as He was on earth; and that, consequently, He has retained the obedience and submission of the most perfect Child toward the best of all mothers. But we must take great pains not to conceive this dependence as any abasement or imperfection in Jesus Christ. For Mary is infinitely below her Son, who is God, and therefore she does not command Him as a mother here below would command her child who is below her. Mary, being altogether transformed into God by grace and by the glory which transforms all the saints into Him, asks nothing, wishes nothing, does nothing contrary to the eternal and immutable will of God. When we read then in the writings of Sts. Bernard, Bernardine, Bonaventure and others that in Heaven and on earth everything, even God Himself, is subject to the Blessed Virgin,[5] they mean that the authority which God has been well pleased to give her is so great that

it seems as if she had the same power as God; and that her prayers and petitions are so powerful with God that they always pass for commandments with His Majesty, who never resists the prayer of His dear Mother, because she is always humble and conformed to His will.

If Moses, by the force of his prayer, stayed the anger of God against the Israelites in a manner so powerful that the most high and infinitely merciful Lord, being unable to resist him, told him to let Him alone that He might be angry with and punish that rebellious people, what must we not, with much greater reason, think of the prayer of the humble Mary, that worthy Mother of God, which is more powerful with His Majesty than the prayers and intercessions of all the angels and saints both in Heaven and on earth?[6]

28. In the Heavens Mary commands the angels and the blessed. As a recompense for her profound humility, God has empowered her and commissioned her to fill with saints the empty thrones from which the apostate angels fell by pride.[7] The will of the Most High, who exalts the humble (*Lk.* 1:52), is that Heaven, earth and Hell bend, with good will or bad will, to the commandments of the humble Mary,[8] whom He has made sovereign of Heaven and earth, general of His armies, treasurer of His treasures, dispenser of His graces, worker of His greatest marvels, restorer of the human race, Mediatrix of men, the exterminator of the enemies of God, and the faithful companion of His grandeurs and triumphs.

29. God the Father wishes to have children by Mary till the consummation of the world; and He speaks to her these words: "Dwell in Jacob" (*Ecclus.* 24:13); that

is to say: Make your dwelling and residence in My pre-
destined children, prefigured by Jacob, and not in the
reprobate children of the devil, prefigured by Esau.

30. Just as in the natural and corporal generation
of children there are a father and a mother, so in the
supernatural and spiritual generation there are a
Father, who is God, and a Mother, who is Mary. All
the true children of God, the predestinate, have God
for their Father and Mary for their Mother. He who
has not Mary for his Mother has not God for his
Father. This is the reason why the reprobate, such as
heretics, schismatics and others, who hate our Blessed
Lady or regard her with contempt and indifference,
have not God for their Father, however much they
boast of it, simply because they have not Mary for
their Mother. For if they had her for their Mother,
they would love and honor her as a true child
naturally loves and honors the mother who has given
him life.

The most infallible and indubitable sign by which
we may distinguish a heretic, a man of bad doctrine, a
reprobate, from one of the predestinate, is that the
heretic and the reprobate have nothing but contempt
and indifference for Our Lady, endeavoring by their
words and examples to diminish the worship and love
of her, openly or hiddenly, and sometimes by mis-
representation. Alas! God the Father has not told
Mary to dwell in them, for they are Esaus.

31. God the Son wishes to form Himself, and, so to
speak, to incarnate Himself in His members every
day, by His dear Mother, and He says to her: "Take
Israel for your inheritance." (*Ecclus.* 24:13). It is as if
He had said: God the Father has given Me for an inheritance all the nations of the earth, all men, good

and bad, predestinate and reprobate. The ones I will lead with a rod of gold, and the others with a rod of iron. Of the ones, I will be the Father and the Advocate; of the others, the Just Punisher; and of all, the Judge. But as for you, My dear Mother, you shall have for your heritage and possession only the predestinate, prefigured by Israel; and as their Mother, you shall bring them forth and take care of them; and as their sovereign, you shall conduct them, govern them and defend them.

32. "This man and that man is born in her" (*Ps.* 86:5), says the Holy Ghost through the Royal Psalmist. According to the explanation of some of the Fathers,[9] the first man that is born in Mary is the Man-God, Jesus Christ; the second is a mere man, the child of God and Mary by adoption. If Jesus Christ, the Head of men, is born in her, then the predestinate, who are the members of that Head, ought also to be born in her, by a necessary consequence. One and the same mother does not bring forth into the world the head without the members, or the members without the head; for this would be a monster of nature. So in like manner, in the order of grace, the head and the members are born of one and the same Mother; and if a member of the Mystical Body of Jesus Christ—that is to say, one of the predestinate—were born of any other mother than Mary, who has produced the Head, he would not be one of the predestinate, nor a member of Jesus Christ, but simply a monster in the order of grace.

33. Besides this, Jesus being at present as much as ever the fruit of Mary—as Heaven and earth repeat thousands and thousands of times a day, "and blessed is the fruit of thy womb, Jesus"—it is certain that

Jesus Christ is, for each man in particular who possesses Him, as truly the fruit and the work of Mary as He is for the whole world in general; so that if any one of the faithful has Jesus Christ formed in his heart, he can say boldly, "All thanks be to Mary! What I possess is her effect and her fruit, and without her I should never have had it." We can apply to her more than St. Paul applied to himself the words: "I am in labor again with all the children of God, until Jesus Christ my Son be formed in them in the fullness of His age." (Cf. *Gal.* 4:19).

St. Augustine, surpassing himself, and going beyond all I have yet said, affirms that all the predestinate, in order to be conformed to the image of the Son of God, are in this world hidden in the womb of the most holy Virgin, where they are guarded, nourished, brought up and made to grow by that good Mother until she has brought them forth to glory after death, which is properly the day of their birth, as the Church calls the death of the just. O mystery of grace, unknown to the reprobate, and but little known even to the predestinate!

34. God the Holy Ghost wishes to form elect for Himself in her and by her, and He says to her: "Strike the roots," My Well-beloved and My Spouse, "of all your virtues in My elect" (*Ecclus.* 24:13), in order that they may grow from virtue to virtue and from grace to grace. I took so much complacence in you when you lived on earth in the practice of the most sublime virtues, that I desire still to find you on earth, without your ceasing to be in Heaven. For this end, reproduce yourself in My elect, that I may behold in them with complacence the roots of your invincible faith, of your profound humility, of your universal

mortification, of your sublime prayer, of your ardent charity, of your firm hope and of all your virtues. You are always My spouse, as faithful, as pure and as fruitful as ever. Let your faith give Me My faithful, your purity, My virgins, and your fertility, My temples and My elect.

35. When Mary has struck her roots in a soul, she produces there marvels of grace, which she alone can produce, because she alone is the fruitful Virgin who never has had, and never will have, her equal in purity and in fruitfulness.

Mary has produced, together with the Holy Ghost, the greatest thing which has been or ever will be—a God-Man; and she will consequently produce the greatest saints that there will be in the end of time. The formation and the education of the great saints who shall come at the end of the world are reserved for her. For it is only that singular and miraculous Virgin who can produce, in union with the Holy Ghost, singular and extraordinary things.

36. When the Holy Ghost, her Spouse, has found Mary in a soul, He flies there. He enters there in His fullness; He communicates Himself to that soul abundantly, and to the full extent to which it makes room for His spouse. Nay, one of the greatest reasons why the Holy Ghost does not now do startling wonders in our souls is because He does not find there a sufficiently great union with His faithful and inseparable spouse. I say "inseparable" spouse, because since that Substantial Love of the Father and the Son has espoused Mary, in order to produce Jesus Christ, the Head of the elect, and Jesus Christ in the elect, He has never repudiated her, because she has always been fruitful and faithful.

Consequences

I. Mary Is Queen of All Hearts

37. We may evidently conclude, then, from what I have said, first of all, that Mary has received from God a great domination over the souls of the elect; for she cannot make her residence in them as God the Father ordered her to do, and, as their mother, form, nourish and bring them forth to eternal life, and have them as her inheritance and portion, and form them in Jesus Christ and Jesus Christ in them, and strike the roots of her virtues in their hearts and be the inseparable companion of the Holy Ghost in all His works of grace—she cannot, I say, do all these things unless she has a right and a domination over their souls by a singular grace of the Most High, who, having given her power over His only and natural Son, has given it also to her over His adopted children, not only as to their bodies, which would be but a small matter, but also as to their souls.

38. Mary is the Queen of Heaven and earth by grace, as Jesus is the King of them by nature and by conquest. Now, as the kingdom of Jesus Christ consists principally in the heart or the interior of man— according to the words, "The kingdom of God is within you" (*Lk.* 17:21)—in like manner the kingdom of our Blessed Lady is principally in the interior of man; that is to say, his soul. And it is principally in souls that she is more glorified with her Son than in all visible creatures, and so we can call her, as the saints do, the Queen of All Hearts.

II. Mary Is Necessary to Men

39. In the second place we must conclude that, the most holy Virgin being necessary to God by a necessity which we call "hypothetical," in consequence of His will, she is far more necessary to men, in order that they may attain their last end. We must not confuse devotion to the Blessed Virgin with devotions to the other saints, as if devotion to her were not far more necessary than devotion to them, and as if devotion to her were a matter of supererogation.

§ 1. Necessary to all men to attain salvation.

40. The learned and pious Jesuit, Suarez, the erudite and devout Justus Lipsius, doctor of Louvain, and many others have proved invincibly, from the sentiments of the Fathers (among others, St. Augustine, St. Ephrem, deacon of Edessa, St. Cyril of Jerusalem, St. Germanus of Constantinople, St. John Damascene, St. Anselm, St. Bernard, St. Bernardine, St. Thomas and St. Bonaventure), that devotion to our Blessed Lady is necessary to salvation, and that (even in the opinion of Oecolampadius and some other heretics) it is an infallible mark of reprobation to have no esteem and love for the holy Virgin; while on the other hand, it is an infallible mark of predestination to be entirely and truly devoted to her.[10]

41. The figures and words of the Old and New Testaments prove this. The sentiments and the examples of the saints confirm it. Reason and experience teach and demonstrate it. Even the devil and his crew, constrained by the force of truth, have often been obliged to avow it in spite of themselves. Among all

the passages of the holy Fathers and Doctors, of which I have made an ample collection in order to prove this truth, I shall for brevity's sake quote but one: "To be devout to you, O holy Virgin," says St. John Damascene, "is an arm of salvation which God gives to those whom He wishes to save."

42. I could bring forward here many anecdotes which prove the same thing, and among others one which is related in the chronicles of St. Francis. This same saint saw in ecstasy a great ladder ascending into Heaven, at the top of which stood the Blessed Virgin and by which it was shown him he must ascend to reach Heaven. There is another related in the chronicles of St. Dominic. There was an unfortunate heretic near Carcassonne, where St. Dominic was preaching the Rosary, who was possessed by a legion of fifteen thousand devils. These evil spirits were compelled, to their confusion, by the command of our Blessed Lady, to avow many great and consoling truths touching devotion to the Blessed Virgin; and they did this with so much force and so much clearness that it is impossible to read this authentic account and the eulogy which the devil made, in spite of himself, of devotion to the most holy Virgin Mary, without shedding tears of joy, however lukewarm we may be in our devotion to her.

§ 2. Still more necessary to those called to a special perfection.

43. If devotion to the most holy Virgin Mary is necessary to all men simply for working out their salvation, it is still more so for those who are called to any special perfection; and I do not think anyone can ac-

quire an intimate union with Our Lord and a perfect fidelity to the Holy Ghost without a very great union with the most holy Virgin, and a great dependence on her assistance.

44. It is Mary alone who has found grace before God (*Lk*. 1:30) without the aid of any other mere creature; it is only through her that all those who have since found grace before God have found it at all; and it is only through her that all those who shall come afterward shall find it. She was full of grace when she was greeted by the Archangel Gabriel (*Lk*. 1:28), and she was superabundantly filled with grace by the Holy Ghost when He covered her with His unspeakable shadow (*Lk*. 1:35); and she has so augmented this double plenitude from day to day and from moment to moment that she has reached a point of grace immense and inconceivable—in such wise that the Most High has made her the sole treasurer of His treasures and the sole dispenser of His graces to ennoble, to exalt and to enrich whom she wishes; to give entry to whom she wills into the narrow way of Heaven; to bring whom she wills, and in spite of all obstacles, through the narrow gate of life; and to give the throne, the scepter and the crown of king to whom she wills. Jesus is everywhere and always the Fruit and the Son of Mary; and Mary is everywhere the veritable tree who bears the Fruit of life, and the true Mother who produces it.[11]

45. It is Mary alone to whom God has given the keys of the cellars (*Cant*. 1:3) of divine love and the power to enter into the most sublime and secret ways of perfection, and the power likewise to make others enter in there also. It is Mary alone who has given to the miserable children of Eve, the faithless, entry into

the terrestrial paradise; that they may walk there agreeably with God, hide there securely against their enemies, feed themselves there deliciously, without further fear of death, on the fruit of the trees of life and of the knowledge of good and evil, and drink in long draughts the heavenly waters of that fair fountain which gushes forth there with abundance; or rather, since she is herself that terrestrial paradise, that virgin and blessed earth from which Adam and Eve, the sinners, have been driven, she gives no entry there except to those whom it is her pleasure to make saints.

46. All the rich among the people, to make use of an expression of the Holy Ghost (*Ps.* 44:13) according to the explanation of St. Bernard—all the rich among the people shall supplicate her face from age to age, and particularly at the end of the world; that is to say, the greatest saints, the souls richest in graces and virtues, shall be the most assiduous in praying to our Blessed Lady, and in having her always present as their perfect model for imitation and their powerful aid for help.

§ 3. Especially necessary to the great saints of the latter times.

47. I have said that this would come to pass, particularly at the end of the world and indeed presently,[12] because the Most High with His holy Mother has to form for Himself great saints who shall surpass most of the other saints in sanctity as much as the cedars of Lebanon outgrow the little shrubs, as has been revealed to a holy soul whose life has been written by M. de Renty.

48. These great souls, full of grace and zeal, shall

be chosen to match themselves against the enemies of God, who shall rage on all sides; and they shall be singularly devout to our Blessed Lady, illuminated by her light, strengthened with her nourishment, led by her spirit, supported by her arm and sheltered under her protection, so that they shall fight with one hand and build with the other. With the one hand they shall fight, overthrow and crush the heretics with their heresies, the schismatics with their schisms, the idolaters with their idolatries and the sinners with their impieties. With the other hand they shall build (*Esd.* 4:7) the temple of the true Solomon[13] and the mystical city of God,[14] that is to say, the most holy Virgin, called by the Fathers the "Temple of Solomon" and the "City of God." By their words and their examples they shall draw the whole world to true devotion to Mary. This shall bring upon them many enemies, but shall also bring many victories and much glory for God alone. This is what God revealed to St. Vincent Ferrer, the great apostle of his age, as he has sufficiently noted in one of his works.

This is what the Holy Ghost seems to have prophesied in the Fifty-eighth Psalm: "And they shall know that God will rule Jacob and all the ends of the earth; they shall return at evening and shall suffer hunger like dogs and shall go round about the city." (*Ps.* 58:14-15). This city which men shall find at the end of the world to convert themselves in, and to satisfy the hunger they have for justice, is the most holy Virgin, who is called by the Holy Ghost the "City of God." (*Ps.* 86:3).

—Article Three—
PROVIDENTIAL FUNCTION OF MARY
IN THE LATTER TIMES

49. It was through Mary that the salvation of the world was begun, and it is through Mary that it must be consummated. Mary hardly appeared at all in the first coming of Jesus Christ, in order that men, as yet but little instructed and enlightened on the Person of her Son, should not remove themselves from Him in attaching themselves too strongly and too grossly to her. This would have apparently taken place if she had been known, because of the admirable charms which the Most High had bestowed even upon her exterior. This is so true that St. Denis the Areopagite tells us in his writings that when he saw our Blessed Lady he would have taken her for a divinity, because of her secret charms and incomparable beauty, had not the faith in which he was well established taught him the contrary.[15] But in the second coming of Jesus Christ, Mary has to be made known and revealed by the Holy Ghost in order that, through her, Jesus Christ may be known, loved and served. The reasons which moved the Holy Ghost to hide His spouse during her life, and to reveal her but very little since the preaching of the Gospel, subsist no longer.

I. Existence of This Function and Reasons for It

50. God, then, wishes to reveal and make known Mary, the masterpiece of His hands, in these latter times:

§ 1. Because she hid herself in this world and put herself lower than the dust by her profound humility, having obtained from God and from His Apostles and Evangelists that she should not be made manifest.

§ 2. Because, as she is the masterpiece of the hands of God, as well here below by grace as in Heaven by glory, He wishes to be glorified and praised in her by those who are living upon the earth.

§ 3. As she is the dawn which precedes and reveals the Sun of Justice, who is Jesus Christ, she must be seen and recognized in order that Jesus Christ may also be.

§ 4. Being the way by which Jesus came to us the first time, she will also be the way by which He will come the second time, though not in the same manner.

§ 5. Being the sure means and the straight and immaculate way to go to Jesus Christ and to find Him perfectly, it is by her that the souls who are to shine forth especially in sanctity have to find Our Lord. He who shall find Mary shall find life (*Prov.* 8:35), that is, Jesus Christ, who is the Way, the Truth and the Life. (*Jn.* 14:6). But no one can find Mary who does not seek her; and no one can seek her who does not know her; for we cannot seek or desire an unknown object. It is necessary, then, for the greater knowledge and glory of the Most Holy Trinity, that Mary should be more than ever known.

§ 6. Mary must shine forth more than ever in mercy, in might and in grace, in these latter times: in mercy, to bring back and lovingly receive the poor strayed sinners who shall be converted and shall return to the Catholic Church; in might, against the enemies of God, idolaters, schismatics, Mahometans, Jews and souls hardened in impiety, who shall rise in terrible revolt against God to seduce all those who shall oppose them and to make them fall by promises and threats; and finally, she must shine forth in grace, in order to animate and sustain the valiant soldiers and faithful servants of Jesus Christ, who shall battle for His interests.

§ 7. And lastly, Mary must be terrible to the devil and his crew, as an army ranged in battle, principally in these latter times,[16] because the devil, knowing that he has but little time, and now less than ever, to destroy souls, will every day redouble his efforts and his combats. He will presently raise up cruel persecutions and will put terrible snares before the faithful servants and true children of Mary, whom it gives him more trouble to conquer than it does to conquer others.

II. Exercise of This Function

§ 1. In the struggle against Satan.

51. It is principally of these last and cruel persecutions of the devil, which shall go on increasing daily till the reign of Antichrist, that we ought to understand that first and celebrated prediction and curse of God pronounced in the terrestrial paradise against the serpent. It is to our purpose to explain this here for the glory of the most holy Virgin, for the salvation of her children and for the confusion of the devil: "I will put enmities between thee and the woman and thy seed and her seed; she shall crush thy head, and thou shalt lie in wait for her heel." (*Gen.* 3:15).

52. God has never made and formed but one enmity; but it is an irreconcilable one, which shall endure and grow even to the end. It is between Mary, His worthy Mother, and the devil—between the children and the

servants of the Blessed Virgin, and the children and
tools of Lucifer. The most terrible of all the enemies
which God has set up against the devil is His holy
Mother Mary. He has inspired her, even since the days
of the earthly paradise—though she existed then only
in His idea—with so much hatred against that cursed
enemy of God, with so much ingenuity in unveiling the
malice of that ancient serpent, with so much power to
conquer, to overthrow and to crush that proud, impious
rebel, that he fears her not only more than all angels
and men, but in a sense more than God Himself. Not
that the anger, the hatred and the power of God are not
infinitely greater than those of the Blessed Virgin, for
the perfections of Mary are limited; but first, because
Satan, being proud, suffers infinitely more from being
beaten and punished by a little and humble handmaid
of God, and her humility humbles him more than the
divine power; and secondly, because God has given
Mary such great power against the devils that—as they
have often been obliged to confess, in spite of themselves, by the mouths of the possessed—they fear one of
her sighs for a soul more than the prayers of all the
saints, and one of her threats against them more than all
other torments.

53. What Lucifer has lost by pride, Mary has
gained by humility. What Eve has damned and lost by
disobedience, Mary has saved by obedience. Eve, in
obeying the serpent, has destroyed all her children
together with herself, and has delivered them to him;
Mary, in being perfectly faithful to God, has saved all
her children and servants together with herself, and
has consecrated them to His Majesty.

54. God has not only set an enmity, but enmities,
not simply between Mary and the devil, but between

the race of the holy Virgin and the race of the devil; that is to say, God has set enmities, antipathies and secret hatreds between the true children and servants of Mary and the children and slaves of the devil. They have no love for each other. They have no sympathy for each other. The children of Belial, the slaves of Satan, the friends of the world (for it is the same thing) have always up to this time persecuted those who belong to our Blessed Lady, and will in the future persecute them more than ever; just as Cain, of old, persecuted his brother Abel, and Esau his brother Jacob, who are the figures of the reprobate and the predestinate. But the humble Mary will always have the victory over that proud spirit, and so great a victory that she will go so far as to crush his head, where his pride dwells. She will always discover the malice of the serpent. She will always lay bare his infernal plots and dissipate his diabolical councils, and even to the end of time will guard her faithful servants from his cruel claw.

But the power of Mary over all the devils will especially shine forth in the latter times, when Satan will lay his snares against her heel: that is to say, her humble slaves and her poor children, whom she will raise up to make war against him. They shall be little and poor in the world's esteem, and abased before all like the heel, trodden underfoot and persecuted as the heel is by the other members of the body. But in return for this they shall be rich in the grace of God, which Mary shall distribute to them abundantly. They shall be great and exalted before God in sanctity, superior to all other creatures by their lively zeal, and so well sustained with God's assistance that, with the humility of their heel, in union with Mary, they shall crush the head of the devil and cause Jesus Christ to triumph.

§ 2. In the formation of the apostles of the latter times.

55. In a word, God wishes that His holy Mother should be at present more known, more loved, more honored than she has ever been. This, no doubt, will take place if the predestinate enter, with the grace and light of the Holy Ghost, into the interior and perfect practice which I will disclose to them shortly. Then they will see clearly, as far as faith allows, that beautiful Star of the Sea. They will arrive happily in harbor, following its guidance, in spite of the tempests and the pirates. They will know the grandeurs of that Queen and will consecrate themselves entirely to her service as subjects and slaves of love. They will experience her sweetness and her maternal goodness, and they will love her tenderly like well-beloved children. They will know the mercies of which she is full, and the need they have of her help; and they will have recourse to her in all things, as to their dear advocate and Mediatrix with Jesus Christ. They will know what is the surest, the easiest, the shortest and the most perfect means of going to Jesus Christ; and they will give themselves to Mary, body and soul, without reserve, that they may thus belong entirely to Jesus Christ.

56. But who shall those servants, slaves and children of Mary be?

They shall be the ministers of the Lord who, like a burning fire, shall kindle the fire of divine love everywhere.

They shall be "like sharp arrows in the hand of the powerful" Mary to pierce her enemies. (*Ps.* 126:4).

They shall be the sons of Levi, well purified by the fire of great tribulation, and closely adhering to God (*1 Cor.* 6:17), who shall carry the gold of love in their heart, the incense of prayer in their spirit, and the myrrh of mortification in their body. They shall be everywhere the good odor of Jesus Christ to the poor and to the little, while at the same time, they shall be an odor of death to the great, to the rich and to the proud worldlings.

57. They shall be clouds thundering and flying through the air at the least breath of the Holy Ghost; who, detaching themselves from everything and troubling themselves about nothing, shall shower forth the rain of the Word of God and of life eternal. They shall thunder against sin; they shall storm against the world; they shall strike the devil and his crew; and they shall pierce through and through, for life or for death, with their two-edged sword of the Word of God (*Eph.* 6:17), all those to whom they shall be sent on the part of the Most High.

58. They shall be the true apostles of the latter times, to whom the Lord of Hosts shall give the word and the might to work marvels and to carry off with glory the spoils of His enemies. They shall sleep without gold or silver, and, what is more, without care, in the midst of the other priests, ecclesiastics, and clerics (*Ps.* 67:14); and yet they shall have the silvered wings of the dove to go, with the pure intention of the glory of God and the salvation of souls, wheresoever the Holy Ghost shall call them. Nor shall they leave behind them, in the places where they have preached, anything but the gold of charity, which is the fulfill-

ment of the whole law. (*Rom.* 13:10).

59. In a word, we know that they shall be true disciples of Jesus Christ, walking in the footsteps of His poverty, humility, contempt of the world, charity; teaching the narrow way of God in pure truth, according to the holy Gospel, and not according to the maxims of the world; troubling themselves about nothing; not accepting persons; sparing, fearing and listening to no mortal, however influential he may be. They shall have in their mouths the two-edged sword of the Word of God. They shall carry on their shoulders the bloody standard of the Cross, the Crucifix in their right hand and the Rosary in their left, the sacred Names of Jesus and Mary in their hearts, and the modesty and mortification of Jesus Christ in their own behaviour.[17]

These are the great men who are to come; but Mary is the one who, by order of the Most High, shall fashion them for the purpose of extending His empire over that of the impious, the idolaters and the Mahometans. But when and how shall this be? God alone knows.[18]

As for us, we have but to hold our tongues, to pray, to sigh and to wait: "With expectation I have waited." (*Ps.* 39:2).

NOTES

1. *"Sponsa Spiritus Sancti"* (St. Ildephonsus, *Liber de Corona Virginis,* caput III); *"Sponsus ejus Spiritus veritatis"* (Bellarmin., *Concio 2 super Missus est*).
2. St. Antoninus, *Summa,* p. IV, Tit. 15, cap. 4, no. 5.
3. *Idiota (In contemplatione B.M.V.).*
4. Cf., among others, St. Bernard and St. Bernardine of Siena, whom St. Louis De Montfort quotes further on. (No. 141 and 142).

5. For their exact words cf. no. 76.

6. St. Augustine, *Sermo 208, in Assumptione,* no. 12 *(inter opera Sti. Aug.).*

7. St. Bonaventure, *Speculum B.V.,* lect. XI, no. 6.

8. St. Bonaventure, *Psalt. majus B.V., Cant. instar, can. Trium puerorum.*

9. For instance, Origen and St. Bonaventure; cf. no. 141.

10. In his classic work entitled *The Glories of Mary,* the great Doctor of the Church, St. Alphonsus Liguori (1696-1787) states that "the intercession of Mary is even necessary to salvation; we say necessary—not absolutely, but morally. This necessity proceeds from the will itself of God, that all graces that He dispenses should pass by the hands of Mary, according to the opinion of St. Bernard, and which we may now with safety call the general opinion of theologians and learned men." (p.129, TAN edition). St. Alphonsus quotes St. Bernardine of Siena's words to the Blessed Virgin Mary: "O Lady, since thou art the dispenser of all graces, and since the grace of salvation can only come through thy hands, our salvation depends on thee." (p. 144).

11. Cf. no. 33.

12. St. Louis De Montfort may have believed, as many people of his time did, that the end of the world was at hand; perhaps, however, all he meant was that this would take place particularly at the end of the world, but would begin soon or presently. As a matter of fact, the century following the one in which he lived was one of increased Marian study and devotion.

13. *Idiota, De B.V.,* pars XVI, contempl. 7. *(S.A.,* X, 367). (The abbreviation *S.A.* refers to the *Summa Aurea*).

14. St. Augustine, *Enarratio in Ps.* 142, no. 3 *(S.A.,* IX, 1012).

15. *S.A.,* 842 *(Epistola ad Paulum).* Unauthentic.

16. It is worthy of note that today the increased efforts of the forces of evil are being countered by a corresponding increase of devotion to the Blessed Virgin, as evidenced by the remarkable growth of the Legion of Mary and the renewed interest in the Sodality of the Blessed Virgin.

17. Cf. prayer of St. Louis De Montfort asking God for missionaries for his Company of Mary (Montfort Fathers).

18. These words show that St. Louis De Montfort himself did not know all the circumstances of his own prophecy concerning the latter times.

Chapter II

FUNDAMENTAL TRUTHS
OF DEVOTION
TO THE BLESSED VIRGIN

60. Having spoken thus far of the necessity of devotion to the most holy Virgin, I must now show in what this devotion consists. This I will do, with God's help, after I shall have first laid down some fundamental truths which shall throw light on that grand and solid devotion which I desire to disclose.

—First Truth—
JESUS CHRIST IS THE LAST END
OF DEVOTION TO MARY

61. Jesus Christ our Saviour, true God and true Man, ought to be the last end of all our other devotions, else they are false and delusive. Jesus Christ is the Alpha and the Omega,[1] the beginning and the end, of all things. We labor not, as the Apostle says, except to render every man perfect in Jesus Christ; because it is in Him alone that the whole plenitude of the Divinity dwells together with all the other plenitudes of graces, virtues and perfections. It is in Him alone that we have been blessed with all spiritual benediction; and He is our only Master, who has to teach us; our only Lord on whom we ought to depend; our only Head to whom we must be united; our only Model to whom we should conform ourselves; our only Physi-

cian who can heal us; our only Shepherd who can feed us; our only Way who can lead us; our only Truth whom we must believe; our only Life who can animate us; and our only All in all things who can satisfy us. There has been no other name given under Heaven, except the name of Jesus, by which we can be saved. God has laid no other foundation of our salvation, our perfection or our glory, than Jesus Christ. Every building which is not built on that firm rock is founded upon the moving sand, and sooner or latter infallibly will fall. Every one of the faithful who is not united to Him, as a branch to the stock of the vine, shall fall, shall wither, and shall be fit only to be cast into the fire. Outside of Him there exists nothing but error, falsehood, iniquity, futility, death and damnation. But if we are in Jesus Christ and Jesus Christ is in us, we have no condemnation to fear. Neither the angels of Heaven nor the men of earth nor the devils of Hell nor any other creature can injure us; because they cannot separate us from the love of God, which is in Jesus Christ. By Jesus Christ, with Jesus Christ, in Jesus Christ, we can do all things; we can render all honor and glory to the Father in the unity of the Holy Ghost;[2] we can become perfect ourselves, and be to our neighbor a good odor of eternal life. (*2 Cor.* 2:15-16).

62. If, then, we establish solid devotion to our Blessed Lady, it is only to establish more perfectly devotion to Jesus Christ, and to provide an easy and secure means for finding Jesus Christ. If devotion to Our Lady removed us from Jesus Christ, we should have to reject it as an illusion of the devil; but so far from this being the case, devotion to Our Lady is, on the contrary, necessary for us—as I have already

shown, and will show still further hereafter—as a means of finding Jesus Christ perfectly, of loving Him tenderly, of serving Him faithfully.

63. I here turn for one moment to Thee, O sweet Jesus, to complain lovingly to Thy Divine Majesty that the greater part of Christians, even the most learned, do not know the necessary union there is between Thee and Thy holy Mother. Thou, Lord, art always with Mary, and Mary is always with Thee, and she cannot be without Thee, else she would cease to be what she is. She is so transformed into Thee by grace that she lives no more, she is as though she were not. It is Thou only, my Jesus, who livest and reignest in her more perfectly than in all the angels and the blessed. Ah! If we knew the glory and the love which Thou receivest in this admirable creature, we should have very different thoughts both of Thee and her from what we have now. She is so intimately united with Thee that it were easier to separate the light from the sun, the heat from the fire; nay, it were easier to separate from Thee all the angels and the saints than the divine Mary, because she loves Thee more ardently and glorifies Thee more perfectly than all the other creatures put together.

64. After that, my sweet Master, is it not an astonishingly pitiable thing to see the ignorance and the darkness of all men here below in regard to Thy holy Mother? I speak not so much of idolaters and pagans, who, knowing Thee not, care not to know her. I speak not even of heretics and schismatics, who care not to be devout to Thy holy Mother, being separated as they are from Thee and Thy holy Church; but I speak of Catholic Christians, and even of doctors among Catholics,[3] who make profession of teaching

truths to others, and yet know not Thee nor Thy holy Mother, except in a speculative, dry, barren and indifferent manner. These gentlemen speak but rarely of Thy holy Mother and of the devotion we ought to have to her, because they fear, so they say, lest we should abuse it, and do some injury to Thee in honoring Thy holy Mother too much. If they hear or see anyone devout to our Blessed Lady, speaking often of his devotion to that good Mother in a tender, strong and persuasive way, and as a secure means without delusion, as a short road without danger, as an immaculate way without imperfection, and as a wonderful secret for finding and loving Thee perfectly, they cry out against him, and give him a thousand false reasons by way of proving to him that he ought not to talk so much of our Blessed Lady; that there are great abuses in that devotion; and that we must direct our energies to destroy these abuses, and to speak of Thee, rather than to incline the people to devotion to our Blessed Lady, whom they already love sufficiently.

We hear them sometimes speak of devotion to our Blessed Lady, not for the purpose of establishing it and persuading men to embrace it, but to destroy the abuses which are made of it; and all the while these teachers are without piety or tender devotion toward Thyself, simply because they have none for Mary. They regard the Rosary and the Scapular as devotions proper for weak and ignorant minds, without which men can save themselves; and if there falls into their hands any poor client of Our Lady who says his Rosary, or has any other practice of devotion toward her, they soon change his spirit and his heart. Instead of the Rosary, they counsel him the seven Penitential

Psalms. Instead of devotion to the holy Virgin, they counsel him devotion to Jesus Christ.

O my sweet Jesus, do these people have Thy spirit? Do they please Thee in acting thus? Does it please Thee when, for fear of displeasing Thee, we neglect doing our utmost to please Thy Mother? Does devotion to Thy holy Mother hinder devotion to Thyself? Does she attribute to herself the honor we pay her? Does she head a faction of her own? Is she a stranger who has no connection with Thee? Does it displease Thee that we should try to please her? Do we separate or alienate ourselves from Thy love by giving ourselves to her and honoring her?

65. Yet, my sweet Master, the greater part of the learned could not discourage devotion to Thy holy Mother more, and could not show more indifference to it, even if all that I have just said were true. Thus have they been punished for their pride! Keep me, Lord, keep me from their sentiments and their practices, and give me some share of the sentiments of gratitude, esteem, respect and love which Thou hast in regard to Thy holy Mother, so that the more I imitate and follow her, the more I may love and glorify Thee.

66. So, as if up to this point I had still said nothing in honor of Thy holy Mother, "give me now the grace to praise Thee worthily," in spite of all her enemies, who are Thine as well; and grant me to say loudly with the saints, "Let not that man presume to look for the mercy of God who offends His holy Mother."

67. Make me love Thee ardently, so that I may obtain of Thy mercy a true devotion to Thy holy Mother, and inspire the whole earth with it; and for that end, receive the burning prayer which I offer to Thee with St. Augustine[4] and Thy other true friends:

"Thou art Christ, my holy Father, my tender God, my great King, my good Shepherd, my one Master, my best Helper, my most Beautiful and my Beloved, my living Bread, my Priest forever, my Leader to my country, my true Light, my holy Sweetness, my straight Way, my excellent Wisdom, my pure Simplicity, my pacific Harmony, my whole Guard, my good Portion, my everlasting Salvation.

"Christ Jesus, my sweet Lord, why have I ever loved, why in my whole life have I ever desired anything except Thee, Jesus my God? Where was I when I was not in Thy mind with Thee? Now, from this time forth, do ye, all my desires, grow hot, and flow out upon the Lord Jesus; run, ye have been tardy thus far; hasten whither ye are going; seek whom ye are seeking. O Jesus, may he who loves Thee not, be anathema; may he who loves Thee not, be filled with bitterness!

"O sweet Jesus, may every good feeling that is fitted for Thy praise, love Thee, delight in Thee, admire Thee. God of my heart and my Portion, Christ Jesus, may my heart faint away in spirit and mayest Thou be my life within me! May the live coal of Thy love grow hot within my spirit, and break forth into a perfect fire; may it burn incessantly on the altar of my heart; may it glow in my innermost being; may it blaze in hidden recesses of my soul; and in the day of my consummation, may I be found consummated with Thee. Amen."

—Second Truth—
WE BELONG TO JESUS AND MARY
AS THEIR SLAVES

68. We must conclude, from what Jesus Christ is with regard to us, that, as the Apostle says (*1 Cor.*

6:19-20), we do not belong to ourselves but are entirely His, as His members and His slaves, whom He has bought at an infinitely dear price, the price of all His Blood. Before Baptism we belonged to the devil, as his slaves; but Baptism has made us true slaves of Jesus Christ, who have no right to live, to work or to die, except to bring forth fruit for that God-Man (*Rom.* 7:4); to glorify Him in our bodies and to let Him reign in our souls, because we are His conquest, His acquired people and His inheritance. It is for the same reason that the Holy Ghost compares us: (1) to trees planted along the waters of grace, in the field of the Church, who ought to bring forth their fruit in their seasons; (2) to the branches of a vine of which Jesus Christ is the stock, and which must yield good grapes; (3) to a flock of which Jesus Christ is the Shepherd, and which is to multiply and give milk; (4) to a good land of which God is the Husbandman, in which the seed multiplies itself and brings forth thirtyfold, sixtyfold and a hundredfold.(*Ps.* 1:3; *Jn.* 15:2; 10:11; *Matt.* 13:8). Jesus Christ cursed the unfruitful fig tree (*Matt.* 21:19), and pronounced sentence against the useless servant who had not made any profit on his talent. (*Matt.* 25:24-30). All this proves to us that Jesus Christ wishes to receive some fruits from our wretched selves, namely our good works, because those works belong to Him alone: "Created in good works, in Christ Jesus" (*Eph.* 2:10)—which words of the Holy Ghost show that Jesus Christ is the sole beginning, and ought to be the sole end, of all our good works, and also that we ought to serve Him, not as servants for wages, but as slaves of love. I will explain what I mean.

69. Here on earth there are two ways of belonging

to another and of depending on his authority: namely, simple service and slavery, whence we derive the words "servant" and "slave."

By common service among Christians a man engages himself to serve another during a certain time, at a certain rate of wages or of recompense.

By slavery a man is entirely dependent on another during his whole life, and must serve his master without claiming any wages or reward, just as one of his beasts, over which he has the right of life and death.

70. There are three sorts of slavery:[5] a slavery of nature, a slavery of constraint and a slavery of will. All creatures are slaves of God in the first sense: "The earth is the Lord's and the fullness thereof" (*Ps.* 23:1); the demons and the damned are slaves in the second sense; the just and the saints in the third. Because by slavery of the will we make choice of God and His service above all things, even though nature did not oblige us to do so, slavery of the will is the most perfect and most glorious to God, who beholds the heart (*1 Kg.* 16:7), claims the heart (*Prov.* 23:26), and calls Himself the God of the heart (*Ps.* 72:26), that is, of the loving will.

71. There is an entire difference between a servant and a slave:

§ 1. A servant does not give all he is, all he has and all he can acquire, by himself or by another, to his master; but the slave gives himself whole and entire to his master, all he has and all he can acquire, without any exception.

§ 2. The servant demands wages for the services which he performs for his master; but the slave can demand nothing, whatever assiduity, whatever industry, whatever energy he may have at his work.

§ 3. The servant can leave his master when he pleases, or at least when the time of his service expires; but the slave has no right to quit his master at will.

§ 4. The master of the servant has no right of life and death over him, so that if he should kill him like one of his beasts of burden, he would commit an unjust homicide; but the master of the slave has by law a right of life and death over him,[6] so that he may sell him to anybody he likes, or kill him as if he stood on the same level as one of his horses.

§ 5. Lastly, the servant is only for a time in his master's service; the slave, always.

72. There is nothing among men which makes us belong to another more than slavery. There is nothing among Christians which makes us more absolutely belong to Jesus Christ and His holy Mother than the slavery of the will, according to the example of Jesus Christ Himself, who took on Himself the form of a slave for love of us (*Phil.* 2:7); and also according to the example of the holy Virgin, who called herself the servant and slave of the Lord. (*Lk.* 1:38). The Apostle calls himself, as by a title of honor, "the slave of Christ."[7] Christians are often so called in the Holy Scriptures; and the word for the designation, *"servus,"* as a great man has truly remarked,[8] signified in olden times a slave in the completest sense, because there were no servants then like those of the present day. Masters were served only by slaves or freedmen. This is what the Catechism of the holy Council of Trent, in order to leave no doubt about our being slaves of Jesus Christ, expresses by an unequivocal term, in calling us *mancipia Christi,* "slaves of Jesus Christ."[9]

73. Now that I have given these explanations, I say

that we ought to belong to Jesus Christ, and to serve Him not only as mercenary servants, but as loving slaves who, as a result of their great love, give themselves up to serve Him in the quality of slaves simply for the honor of belonging to Him. Before Baptism we were the slaves of the devil. Baptism has made us the slaves of Jesus Christ: Christians must needs be either the slaves of the devil or the slaves of Jesus Christ.

74. What I say absolutely of Jesus Christ, I say relatively of Our Lady. Since Jesus Christ chose her for the inseparable companion of His life, of His death, of His glory and of His power in Heaven and upon earth, He gave her by grace, relatively to His Majesty, all the same rights and privileges which He possesses by nature. "All that is fitting to God by nature is fitting to Mary by grace," say the saints; so that, according to them, Mary and Jesus, having but the same will and the same power, have also the same subjects, servants and slaves.[10]

75. We may, therefore, following the sentiments of the saints and of many great men, call ourselves and make ourselves the loving slaves of the most holy Virgin, in order to be, by that very means, the more perfectly the slaves of Jesus Christ. Our Blessed Lady is the means Our Lord made use of to come to us. She is also the means which we must make use of to go to Him.[11] For she is not like all other creatures who, if we should attach ourselves to them, might rather draw us away from God than draw us near Him. The strongest inclination of Mary is to unite us to Jesus Christ, her Son; and the strongest inclination of the Son is that we should come to Him through His holy Mother. It is to honor and to please Him, just as it would be to do honor and pleasure to a king to

become more perfectly his subject and his slave by making ourselves the slaves of the queen. It is on this account that the holy Fathers, and St. Bonaventure after them, say that Our Lady is the way to go to Our Lord: "The way of coming to Christ is to draw near to her."[12]

76. Moreover, if, as I have said,[13] the holy Virgin is the Queen and Sovereign of Heaven and earth, has she not then as many subjects and slaves as there are creatures?[14] St. Anselm, St. Bernard, St. Bernardine, St. Bonaventure say: "All things, the Virgin included, are subject to the empire of God: Behold, all things, and God included, are subject to the empire of the Virgin." Is it not reasonable that among so many slaves of constraint there should be some of love, who of their own good will, in the quality of slaves, should choose Mary for their Mistress? What! Are men and devils to have their voluntary slaves, and Mary to have none? What! Shall a king hold it to be for his honor that the queen, his companion, should have slaves over whom she has the right of life and death,[15] because the honor and power of the one is the honor and power of the other; and yet are we to think that Our Lord, who as the best of all sons has divided His entire power with His holy Mother, shall take it ill that she too has her slaves? Has He less respect and love for His Mother than Ahasuerus had for Esther, or than Solomon had for Bethsebee? Who shall dare say so, or even think so?

77. But whither is my pen hurrying me? Why am I stopping here to prove a thing so plain? If we do not wish to call ourselves slaves of the Blessed Virgin, what matter? Let us make ourselves, and call ourselves, slaves of Jesus Christ; for that is being the

slave of the holy Virgin, inasmuch as Jesus is the fruit
and the glory of Mary; and it is this very thing which
we do perfectly by the devotion of which we are
hereafter to speak.[16]

—Third Truth—
WE NEED MARY IN ORDER TO
DIE TO OURSELVES

78. Our best actions are ordinarily stained and corrupted by our corrupt nature. When we put clean,
clear water into a vessel which has a foul and evil
smell, or wine into a cask the inside of which has been
tainted by another wine which has been in it, the clear
water and the good wine are spoilt, and readily take
on the bad odor. In like manner, when God puts into
the vessel of our soul, spoilt by original and actual sin,
His graces and heavenly dews, or the delicious wine
of His love, His gifts are ordinarily spoilt and corrupted by the bad leaven and the evil which sin has
left within us. Our actions, even the most sublime and
virtuous, feel the effects of it. It is therefore of great
importance in the acquiring of perfection—which, it
must be remembered, is only acquired by union with
Jesus Christ—to rid ourselves of everything that is
bad within us; otherwise Our Lord, who is infinitely
pure and hates infinitely the least stain upon our
souls, will not unite Himself to us, and will cast us out
from His presence.

79. To rid ourselves of self we must:

§ 1. Thoroughly recognize, by the light of the Holy
Ghost, our inward corruption, our incapacity for every good thing useful for salvation, our weakness in
all things, our inconstancy at all times, our unworthi-

ness of every grace, and our iniquity in every position. The sin of our first father has spoilt us all, soured us, puffed us up and corrupted us, as the leaven sours, puffs up and corrupts the dough into which it is put. The actual sins which we have committed, whether mortal or venial, pardoned though they may be, have nevertheless increased our concupiscence, our weakness, our inconstancy and our corruption, and have left evil remains in our souls.

Our bodies are so corrupted that they are called by the Holy Ghost bodies of sin (*Rom.* 6:6), conceived in sin (*Ps.* 50:7), nourished in sin, and capable of all sin—bodies subject to thousands of maladies, which go on corrupting from day to day, and which engender nothing but disease, vermin and corruption.

Our soul, united to our body, has become so carnal that it is called flesh: "All flesh having corrupted its way." (*Gen.* 6:12). We have nothing for our portion but pride and blindness of spirit, hardness of heart, weakness and inconstancy of soul, concupiscence, revolted passions, and sicknesses in the body. We are naturally prouder than peacocks, more groveling than toads, more vile than unclean animals, more envious than serpents, more gluttonous than hogs, more furious than tigers, lazier than tortoises, weaker than reeds, and more capricious than weathercocks. We have within ourselves nothing but nothingness and sin, and we deserve nothing but the anger of God and everlasting Hell.[17]

80. After this, ought we to be astonished if Our Lord has said that whoever wishes to follow Him must renounce himself and hate his own life, and that whosoever shall love his own life shall lose it, and whosoever shall hate it, shall save it? (*Jn.* 12:25). He

who is infinite Wisdom does not give commandments
without reason, and He has commanded us to hate
ourselves only because we so richly deserve to be
hated. Nothing is worthier of love than God, and
nothing is worthier of hatred than ourselves.

81. § 2. In order to rid ourselves of self, we must
die to ourselves daily. That is to say, we must renounce the operations of the powers of our soul and
of the senses of our body. We must see as if we saw
not, understand as if we understood not, and make use
of the things of this world as if we made no use of
them at all. (*1 Cor.* 7:29-31). This is what St. Paul
calls dying daily. (*1 Cor.* 15:31). "Unless the grain of
wheat falling into the ground die, itself remaineth
alone," and bringeth forth no good fruit. (*Jn.*
12:24-25). If we do not die to ourselves, and if our
holiest devotions do not incline us to this necessary
and useful death, we shall bring forth no fruit worth
anything, and our devotions will become useless. All
our good works will be stained by self-love and our
own will; and this will cause God to hold in abomina-
tion the greatest sacrifices we can make and the best
actions we can do; so that at our death we shall find
our hands empty of virtues and of merits and we shall
not have one spark of pure love, which is only communicated to souls dead to themselves, souls whose
life is hidden with Jesus Christ in God. (*Col.* 3:3).

82. § 3. We must choose, therefore, among all the
devotions to the Blessed Virgin, the one which draws
us most toward this death to ourselves, inasmuch as it
will be the best and the most sanctifying. For we must
not think that all that shines is gold, that all that tastes
sweet is honey, or that all that is easy to do and is
done by the greatest number is the most sanctifying.

As there are secrets of nature by which natural operations are performed more easily, in a short time and at little cost, so also are there secrets in the order of grace by which supernatural operations, such as ridding ourselves of self, filling ourselves with God, and becoming perfect, are performed more easily.

The practice which I am about to disclose is one of these secrets of grace, unknown to the greater number of Christians, known even to few of the devout, and practiced and relished by a lesser number still. But by way of beginning the explanation of this practice, let us consider a fourth truth which is a consequence of the third.

—Fourth Truth—
WE NEED MARY AS OUR MEDIATRIX WITH OUR MEDIATOR, JESUS CHRIST

83. It is more perfect, because it is more humble, not to approach God of ourselves without taking a mediator. Our nature, as I have just shown, is so corrupted that if we rely on our own works, efforts and preparations in order to reach God and please Him, it is certain that our good works will be defiled or be of little weight before God in inducing Him to unite Himself to us and to hear us. It is not without reason that God has given us mediators with His Majesty. He has seen our unworthiness and our incapacity; He has had pity on us; and in order to give us access to His mercies, He has provided us with powerful intercessors with His Grandeur, so that to neglect these mediators, and to draw near to His Holiness directly, and without any recommendation, is to fail in humility. It is to fail in respect toward God, so high and so holy. It is to make less ac-

count of that King of Kings than we should make of a
king or prince of this earth, whom we would not
willingly approach without some friend to speak for us.

84. Our Lord is our advocate and Mediator of
redemption with God the Father. It is through Him
that we ought to pray, in union with the whole
Church, Triumphant and Militant. It is through Him
that we have access to the Majesty of the Father,
before whom we ought never to appear except sustained and clothed with the merits of His Son, just as
the young Jacob came before his father Isaac in the
skins of the kids to receive his blessing.

85. But have we not need of a mediator with the
Mediator Himself? Is our purity great enough to unite
us directly to Him, and by ourselves? Is He not God,
in all things equal to His Father, and consequently the
Holy of Holies, as worthy of respect as His Father? If
through His infinite charity He has made Himself our
bail and our Mediator with God His Father, in order
to appease Him and to pay Him what we owed Him,
are we, on that account, to have less respect and less
fear for His Majesty and His Sanctity?

Let us say boldly with St. Bernard[18] that we have
need of a mediator with the Mediator Himself, and that
it is the divine Mary who is the most capable of filling
that charitable office. It was through her that Jesus
Christ came to us, and it is through her that we must go
to Him. If we fear to go directly to Jesus Christ, our
God, whether because of His infinite greatness or
because of our vileness or because of our sins, let us
boldly implore the aid and intercession of Mary, our
Mother. She is good, she is tender, she has nothing in
her austere and forbidding, nothing too sublime and
too brilliant. In seeing her, we see our pure nature. She

is not the sun, which by the brightness of its rays blinds us because of our weakness; but she is fair and gentle as the moon (*Cant.* 6:9), which receives the light of the sun, and tempers it to make it more suitable to our capacity. She is so charitable that she repels none of those who ask her intercession, no matter how great sinners they have been; for, as the saints say, never has it been heard since the world was the world that anyone has confidently and perseveringly had recourse to our Blessed Lady and yet has been repelled.[19] She is so powerful that none of her petitions has ever been refused. She has but to show herself before her Son to pray to Him, and straightaway He grants her desires, straightaway He receives her prayers. He is always lovingly vanquished by the prayers of His dearest Mother, who bore Him and nourished Him.[20]

86. All this is taken from St. Bernard and St. Bonaventure, so that according to them, we have three steps to mount to go to God: the first, which is nearest to us and the most suited to our capacity, is Mary; the second is Jesus Christ; and the third is God the Father. To go to Jesus, we must go to Mary; she is our mediatrix of intercession. To go to God the Father, we must go to Jesus; for He is our Mediator of redemption. Now the devotion that I am about to bring forward observes this order perfectly.

—Fifth Truth—
WE NEED MARY IN ORDER TO PRESERVE THE GRACES AND TREASURES WE HAVE RECEIVED FROM GOD

87. It is very difficult, considering our weakness and frailty, to preserve in ourselves the graces and treasures

which we have received from God:

§ 1. Because we have this treasure, which is worth more than Heaven and earth put together, in frail vessels, i.e., in a corruptible body and in a weak and inconstant soul, which a mere nothing disturbs and dejects: "We have this treasure in earthen vessels." (*2 Cor.* 4:7).

88. § 2. Because the devils, who are skillful thieves, wish to surprise us unawares, and to strip us. They watch day and night for the favorable moment. For that end they go round about us incessantly to devour us and to snatch from us in one moment, by a sin, all the graces and merits we have gained for many years. Their malice, their experience, their stratagems and their number ought to make us fear this misfortune immensely, especially when we see how many persons fuller of grace than we are, richer in virtues, better founded in experience and far higher exalted in sanctity, have been surprised, robbed and unhappily pillaged. Ah! How many cedars of Lebanon, how many stars of the firmament, have we not seen fall miserably, and in the twinkling of an eye lose all their height and their brightness! Whence comes that sad and curious change? It was not for want of grace, which is wanting to no man; but it was for want of humility. They thought themselves capable of guarding their own treasures. They trusted in themselves, relied upon themselves. They thought their house secure enough, and their coffers strong enough, to keep the precious treasure of grace. It is because of that scarcely perceptible reliance upon themselves, though all the while it seemed to them that they were relying only on the grace of God, that the most just Lord permitted them to be robbed by leaving them to

themselves. Alas! If they had but known the admirable devotion which I will unfold presently, they would have confided their treasure to a Virgin powerful and faithful, who would have kept it for them as if it had been her own possession; nay, who would have even taken it as an obligation of justice on herself to preserve it for them.

89. § 3. It is difficult to persevere in justice because of the strange corruption of the world. The world is now so corrupt it seems inevitable that religious hearts should be soiled, if not by its mud, at least by its dust; so that it has become a kind of miracle for anyone to remain in the midst of that impetuous torrent without being drawn in by it, in the midst of that stormy sea without being drowned in it or stripped by the pirates and the corsairs, in the midst of that pestilent air without being infected by it. It is the Virgin, alone faithful, in whom the serpent has never had part, who works this miracle for those who serve her in that sweet way which I have shortly to unfold.

NOTES

1. The following is taken almost entirely from Holy Scripture; cf. *Apoc.* 1:8; *Eph.* 4:13; *Col.* 2:9; *Matt.* 23:8-10; *Jn.* 13:13; *1 Cor.* 8:6; *Col.* 1:18; *Jn.* 13:15; 10:16; *Acts* 4:12; *1 Cor.* 3:11, etc.
2. Canon of the Mass.
3. We should remember that St. Louis De Montfort wrote this at a time when Jansenism, which opposed devotion to the Blessed Virgin, was flourishing throughout Europe. Even eminent authors were deceived by this heretical sect.
4. *Meditationum* lib. I, cap. XVIII, no. 2 (inter opera Sancti Augustini).
5. St. Thomas, *Summa Theol.,* III, Q. 48, a. 4., corp. et ad 1.
6. By law, i.e., by the ancient civil law of some of those countries

where slavery existed; not by the law of God, nor the law of Moses, nor our modern civil codes, which all condemn such an action. St. Louis De Montfort merely states a fact as it once existed. He prescinds entirely from the question of morality and *wishes only to give an example of the complete dependence of which he is speaking.*

7. *Rom.* 1:1; *Gal.* 1:10; *Phil.* 1:1; *Tit.* 1:1; also cf. *1 Cor.* 7:22; *2 Tim.* 2:24. The insistence of Sts. Paul, Peter, James and Jude on calling themselves slaves of Jesus Christ, shows that there is no opposition between this appellation and the words of Jesus: "I will not call you now servants [slaves] . . . but I have called you friends."

8. Henri Marie Boudon, archdeacon of Evreux, in his book, *Le Saint Esclavage de l'admirable Mère de Dieu,* chapter II.

9. *Catechismus Roman.,* Pars Ia, Caput III, De secundo Symboli articulo (in fine).

10. St. John Damascene, *Sermo 2 in Dormitione B. Mariae.*

11. St. Augustine, *Sermo 113 in Nativit. Domini* (inter opera Sti. Augustini).

12. Psalt. majus B.V. Ps. 117.

13. Cf. no. 38.

14. *Speculum B.M.V.,* lect. III, no. 5.

15. Cf. no. 71, note 6.

16. For a further explanation of this second truth, cf. *La Vie Spirituelle à l'école de St. Louis Marie de Montfort,* by A. Lhoumeau, S.M.M., 1 Partie, ch. IV.

17. St. Louis De Montfort speaks here of our nothingness and impotence in the supernatural order, without the help of grace. Thus he says further on, in no. 83: "Our nature is so corrupted that if we rely on our own works . . . *to reach God. . . .*"

18. *Sermo in Dom. infra octav. Assumptionis,* no. 2.

19. St. Bernard, *Sermo in Dom. infra. oct. Assumptionis,* no. 2.

20. St. Bonaventure, *Speculum B.M.V., lectio* XI.

Chapter III

CHOICE OF TRUE DEVOTION
TO THE BLESSED VIRGIN

90. Having laid down these five truths, let us continue. Today, more than ever, we must take pains in choosing true devotion to our Blessed Lady, because, more than ever before, there are false devotions to our Blessed Lady which are easily mistaken for true ones. The devil, like a false coiner and a subtle and experienced sharper, has already deceived and destroyed so many souls by a false devotion to the Blessed Virgin that he makes a daily use of his diabolical experience to plunge many others by this same way into everlasting perdition; amusing them, lulling them to sleep in sin, under the pretext of some prayers badly said or of some outward practices which he inspires. As a false coiner does not ordinarily counterfeit anything but gold or silver, and very rarely other metals, because they are not worth the trouble, so the evil spirit does not for the most part counterfeit other devotions, but only those to Jesus and Mary—devotion to Holy Communion and to our Blessed Lady— because they are among other devotions what gold and silver are among other metals.

91. It is then very important to recognize, first of all, false devotions to our Blessed Lady, in order to avoid them, and true devotion, in order to embrace it; secondly, which of the many practices of true devotion to our Blessed Lady is the most perfect, the most

agreeable to her, the most glorious to God, and the most sanctifying for ourselves, so that we may adopt that one.

— Article One —
FALSE DEVOTIONS TO THE BLESSED VIRGIN AND FALSE DEVOTEES

92. I find seven kinds of false devotees and false devotions to Our Lady, namely: 1. the critical devotees; 2. the scrupulous devotees; 3. the external devotees; 4. the presumptuous devotees; 5. the inconstant devotees; 6. the hypocritical devotees; 7. the interested devotees.

I. Critical Devotees

93. The critical devotees are, for the most part, proud scholars, rash and self-sufficient spirits, who have at heart some devotion to the holy Virgin, but who criticize nearly all the practices of devotion which simple people pay simply and holily to their good Mother, because these practices do not fall in with their own humor and fancy. They call in doubt all the miracles and pious stories recorded by authors worthy of faith, or drawn from the chronicles of religious orders: narratives which testify to us the mercies and the power of the most holy Virgin. They cannot see, without uneasiness, simple and humble people on their knees before an altar or an image of Our Lady, sometimes at the corner of a street, in order to pray to God there; and they even accuse them of idolatry, as if they adored the wood or the stone. They say that, for their part, they are not fond of

these external devotions, and that they are not so credulous as to believe so many tales and stories that are told about Our Lady. When they are told how admirably the Fathers of the Church praised the Blessed Virgin, they either reply that the Fathers spoke as professional orators, with exaggeration; or they misinterpret their words.[1]

These kinds of false devotees and of proud and worldly people are greatly to be feared. They do an infinite wrong to devotion to Our Lady; and they are but too successful in alienating people from it, under the pretext of destroying its abuses.

II. Scrupulous Devotees

94. The scrupulous devotees are those who fear to dishonor the Son by honoring the Mother, to abase the one in elevating the other. They cannot bear that we should attribute to Our Lady the most just praise which the holy Fathers have given her. It is all they can do to endure that there should be more people before the altar of the Blessed Virgin than before the Blessed Sacrament—as if the one were contrary to the other, as if those who prayed to our Blessed Lady did not pray to Jesus Christ through her. They are unwilling that we should speak so often of Our Lady and address her so frequently.

Here are some of their favorite sayings: "Why so many Rosaries, so many confraternities and so many external devotions to the Blessed Virgin? There is much ignorance in all this. It makes a mummery of our religion. Speak to us of those who are devout to Jesus Christ." (Yet they often name Him without raising their hats—I say this by way of parenthesis.) "We

must have recourse to Jesus Christ; He is our only
Mediator. We must preach Jesus Christ; this is the
solid devotion." What they say is in a certain sense
true, but in the application they make of it, namely, to
hinder devotion to our Blessed Lady, very dangerous;
and it is, under pretext of a greater good, a subtle
snare of the evil one. For the more we honor the
Blessed Virgin, the more we honor Jesus Christ,
because we honor Mary only that we may the more
perfectly honor Jesus, since we go to her only as the
way by which we are to find the end we are seeking,
which is Jesus.

95. The Church, with the Holy Ghost, blesses Our
Lady first, and Our Lord second: "Blessed art thou
among women, and blessed is the fruit of thy womb,
Jesus." It is not that Mary is more than Jesus or even
equal to Him—that would be intolerable heresy; but it
is that, in order to bless Jesus more perfectly, we must
begin by blessing Mary. Let us then say, with all the
true clients of Our Lady, in opposition to these false
scrupulous devotees, "O Mary, thou art blessed
among all women, and blessed is the fruit of thy
womb, Jesus."

III. External Devotees

96. External devotees are persons who make all
devotion to our Blessed Lady consist in outward practices. They have no taste except for the exterior of
this devotion, because they have no interior spirit of
their own. They will say quantities of Rosaries with
the greatest precipitation; they will hear many Masses
distractedly; they will go, without devotion, to proces-
sions; they will enroll themselves in all her confrater-

nities—without amending their lives, without doing any violence to their passions, or without imitating the virtues of that most holy Virgin. They have no love but for the sensible[2] part of devotion, without having any relish for its solidity. If they have not sensible sweetness in their practices, they think they are doing nothing; they get all out of joint, throw everything up, or do everything at random. The world is full of these exterior devotees, and there are no people who are more critical than they of men of prayer, who foster an interior spirit as the essential thing, without, however, disregarding that outward modesty which always accompanies true devotion.

IV. Presumptuous Devotees

97. Presumptuous devotees are sinners abandoned to their passions, or lovers of the world, who under the fair name of Christians and clients of our Blessed Lady conceal pride, avarice, impurity, drunkenness, anger, swearing, detraction, injustice or some other sin. They sleep in peace in the midst of their bad habits, without doing any violence to themselves to correct their faults, under the pretext that they are devout to the Blessed Virgin. They promise themselves that God will pardon them; that they will not be allowed to die without confession; and that they will not be lost eternally because they say the Rosary, because they fast on Saturdays, because they belong to the Confraternity of the Holy Rosary, or wear the Scapular, or are enrolled in other congregations, or they wear the little habit or little chain of Our Lady.

They will not believe us when we tell them that their devotion is only an illusion of the devil and a

pernicious presumption likely to destroy their souls.
They say that God is good and merciful; that He has
not made us to condemn us everlastingly; that no man
is without sin; that they shall not die without confession; that one good act of contrition at the hour of
death is enough; that they are devout to Our Lady,
wear the Scapular, say daily, without fail and without
vanity, seven Our Fathers and seven Hail Marys in
her honor; and that they sometimes say the Rosary
and the Office of Our Lady, besides fasting and other
things. To give authority to all this, and to blind themselves still further, they quote certain stories which
they have heard or read—it does not matter to them
whether they be true or false—relating how people
have died in mortal sin without confession, and then,
because in their lifetime they sometimes said some
prayers or went through some practices of devotion to
Our Lady, how they have been raised to life again in
order to go to confession; or their soul has been
miraculously retained in their bodies till confession;
or through the clemency of the Blessed Virgin they
have obtained from God, at the moment of death,
contrition and pardon of their sins, and so have been
saved; and that they themselves expect similar favors.

98. Nothing in Christianity is more detestable than
this diabolical presumption. For how can we truly say
that we love and honor our Blessed Lady when by our
sins we are pitilessly piercing, wounding, crucifying
and outraging Jesus Christ, her Son? If Mary laid
down a law to herself, to save by her mercy this sort
of people, she would be authorizing crime and helping
crucify and outrage her Son. Who would ever dare
think of such a thing?

99. I say that thus to abuse devotion to Our Lady,

which, after devotion to Our Lord in the Blessed
Sacrament, is the holiest and solidest of all devotions,
is to be guilty of a horrible sacrilege, which, after the
sacrilege of an unworthy Communion, is the greatest
and least pardonable of all sacrileges.

I confess that, in order to be truly devout to our
Blessed Lady, it is not absolutely necessary to be so
holy as to avoid every sin, though this were desirable;
but this much at least is necessary, and I beg you to
lay it well to heart: (1) to have a sincere resolution to
avoid at least all mortal sin, which outrages the
Mother as well as the Son; (2) to do violence to ourselves to avoid sin; (3) to enroll ourselves in confraternities, to say the Rosary or other prayers, to fast on
Saturdays and the like.

100. These good works are likewise wonderfully
useful for the conversion of a sinner, however hardened he may be. If my reader be such a one, even
though he have one foot in the abyss, I would advise
him to practice them, but only on condition that he do
so with the intention of obtaining from God, through
the intercession of the Blessed Virgin, the grace of
contrition and pardon of his sins and the grace to conquer his evil habits, and not to remain quietly in the
state of sin, contrary to his remorse of conscience, the
example of Jesus Christ and the saints and the maxims
of the holy Gospel.

V. Inconstant Devotees

101. The inconstant devotees are those who are
devout to our Blessed Lady by fits and starts. Sometimes they are fervent and sometimes lukewarm.
Sometimes they seem ready to do anything for her,

and then a little afterward, they are not like the same people. They begin by taking up all the devotions to her, and enrolling themselves in the confraternities; and then they do not practice the rules with fidelity. They change like the moon;[3] and Mary puts them under her feet with the crescent, because they are changeable and unworthy to be reckoned among the servants of that faithful Virgin who have for their special graces fidelity and constancy. It were better for such persons not to burden themselves with so many prayers and practices but to choose a few and fulfill them with faithfulness and love, in spite of the world, the devil and the flesh.

VI. Hypocritical Devotees

102. We have still to mention the false devotees to our Blessed Lady who are the hypocritical devotees, who cloak their sins and sinful habits with her mantle, in order to be taken by men for what they are not.

VII. Interested Devotees

103. There are also the interested devotees, who have recourse to Our Lady only to gain some lawsuit, or to avoid some danger, or to be cured of some illness, or for some other similar necessity, without which they would forget her altogether. All these are false devotees, pleasing neither to God nor to His holy Mother.

104. Let us then take great care not to be of the number of the critical devotees, who believe nothing and criticize everything; nor of the scrupulous devotees, who are afraid of being too devout to Our

Lady, out of respect to Our Lord; nor of the exterior devotees, who make all their devotion consist in outward practices; nor of the presumptuous devotees, who, under the pretext of their false devotion to the Blessed Virgin, wallow in their sins; nor of the inconstant devotees, who from levity change their practices of devotion, or give them up altogether, at the least temptation; nor of the hypocritical devotees, who join confraternities and wear the liveries of the Blessed Virgin in order to pass for good people; nor, finally, of the interested devotees, who have recourse to Our Lady only to be delivered from bodily evils, or to obtain temporal goods.

— Article Two —
TRUE DEVOTION
TO THE BLESSED VIRGIN

I. Characteristics

105. After having laid bare and condemned the false devotions to the most holy Virgin, we must, in a few words, give the characteristics of true devotion. It must be: 1. interior, 2. tender, 3. holy, 4. constant, and 5. disinterested.

§ 1. Interior.

106. True devotion to Our Lady is interior; that is, it comes from the mind and the heart. It flows from the esteem we have for her, the high idea we have formed of her greatness, and the love which we have for her.

§ 2. Tender.

107. It is tender; that is, full of confidence in her, like a child's confidence in his loving mother. This confidence makes the soul have recourse to her in all its bodily and mental necessities, with much simplicity, trust and tenderness. It implores the aid of its good Mother at all times, in all places and above all things: in its doubts, that it may be enlightened; in its wanderings, that it may be brought into the right path; in its temptations, that it may be supported; in its weaknesses, that it may be strengthened; in its falls, that it may be lifted up; in its discouragements, that it may be cheered; in its scruples, that they may be taken away; in the crosses, toils and disappointments of life, that it may be consoled under them. In a word, in all the evils of body and mind, the soul ordinarily has recourse to Mary, without fear of annoying her or displeasing Jesus Christ.

§ 3. Holy.

108. True devotion to Our Lady is holy; that is to say, it leads the soul to avoid sin and to imitate the virtues of the Blessed Virgin, particularly her profound humility, her lively faith, her blind obedience, her continual prayer, her universal mortification, her divine purity, her ardent charity, her heroic patience, her angelic sweetness and her divine wisdom. These are the ten principal virtues of the most holy Virgin.

§ 4. Constant.

109. True devotion to Our Lady is constant. It

confirms the soul in good, and does not let it easily abandon its spiritual exercises. It makes it courageous in opposing the world in its fashions and maxims, the flesh in its wearinesses and passions, and the devil in his temptations; so that a person truly devout to our Blessed Lady is neither changeable, irritable, scrupulous nor timid. It is not that such a person does not fall, or change sometimes in the sensible feeling of devotion. But when he falls, he rises again by stretching out his hand to his good Mother. When he loses the taste and relish of devotion, he does not become disturbed because of that; for the just and faithful client of Mary lives by the faith (*Heb.* 10:38) of Jesus and Mary, and not by natural sentiment.

§ 5. Disinterested.

110. Lastly, true devotion to Our Lady is disinterested; that is to say, it inspires the soul not to seek itself but only God, and God in His holy Mother. A true client of Mary does not serve that august Queen from a spirit of lucre and interest, nor for his own good, whether temporal or eternal, corporal or spiritual, but exclusively because she deserves to be served, and God alone in her. He does not love Mary just because she obtains favors for him, or because he hopes she will, but solely because she is so worthy of love. It is on this account that he loves and serves her as faithfully in his disgusts and drynesses as in his sweetnesses and sensible fervors. He loves her as much on Calvary as at the marriage of Cana.

Oh, how agreeable and precious in the eyes of God and of His holy Mother is such a client of our Blessed Lady, who has no self-seeking in his service of her!

But in these days how rare is such a sight! It is that it may be less rare that I have taken my pen in hand to put on paper what I have taught with good results, in public and in private, during my missions for many years.

111. I have now said many things about the most holy Virgin; but I have many more to say, and there are infinitely more which I shall omit, either from ignorance, inability or want of time, in unfolding the plan for forming a true client of Mary and a true disciple of Jesus Christ.

112. Oh, but my labor will have been well expended if this little writing, falling into the hands of a soul of good dispositions—a soul well-born of God and of Mary, and not of blood, nor of the will of the flesh, nor of the will of man (*Jn.* 1:13)—should unfold to him, and should by the grace of the Holy Ghost inspire him with the excellence and the value of that true and solid devotion to our Blessed Lady which I am going presently to describe. If I knew that my guilty blood could serve in engraving upon anyone's heart the truths which I am writing in honor of my true Mother and Sovereign Mistress, of whose children and slaves I am the least, I would use my blood instead of ink to form the letters, in the hope of finding some good souls who, by their fidelity to the practice which I teach, should compensate my dear Mother and Mistress for the losses which she has suffered through my ingratitude and infidelities.

113. I feel myself more than ever encouraged to believe and to hope for the fulfillment of all that I have deeply engraven upon my heart and have asked of God these many years, namely, that sooner or later the Blessed Virgin shall have more children, servants

and slaves of love than ever;[4] and that by this means, Jesus Christ, my dear Master, shall reign in hearts more than ever.

114. I clearly foresee that raging beasts shall come in fury to tear with their diabolical teeth this little writing and him whom the Holy Ghost has made use of to write it—or at least to smother it in the darkness and silence of a coffer, that it may not appear. They shall even attack and persecute those who shall read it and carry it out in practice.[5] But what matter? On the contrary, so much the better! This very foresight encourages me, and makes me hope for great success, that is to say, for a great squadron of brave and valiant soldiers of Jesus and Mary, of both sexes, to combat the world, the devil and corrupted nature, in those more-than-ever perilous times which are about to come. "He who reads, let him understand." (*Matt.* 24:15). "He who can receive it, let him receive it." (*Matt.* 19:12).

II. *Practices*

§ 1. Common practices, both interior and exterior.

115. There are several interior practices of true devotion to the Blessed Virgin. Here are the principal ones, stated compendiously: (1) to honor her as the worthy Mother of God, with the worship of hyperdulia; that is to say, to esteem her and honor her above all the other saints, as the masterpiece of grace, and the first after Jesus Christ, true God and true Man; (2) to meditate on her virtues, her privileges and her actions; (3) to contemplate her grandeurs; (4) to make acts of love, of praise, of gratitude to her; (5) to

invoke her cordially; (6) to offer ourselves to her and unite ourselves with her; (7) to do all our actions with the view of pleasing her; (8) to begin, to continue and to finish all our actions by her, in her, with her and for her, in order that we may do them by Jesus Christ, in Jesus Christ, with Jesus Christ and for Jesus Christ, our Last End. We will presently explain this last practice.[6]

116. True devotion to Our Lady also has several exterior practices, of which the following are the principal ones: (1) to enroll ourselves in her confraternities and enter her congregations; (2) to join the religious orders instituted in her honor; (3) to proclaim her praises; (4) to give alms, to fast and to undergo outward and inward mortifications in her honor; (5) to wear her liveries, such as the Rosary, the Scapular or the little chain; (6) to recite with attention, devotion and modesty the holy Rosary, composed of fifteen decades of Hail Marys in honor of the fifteen principal mysteries of Jesus Christ; or five decades, which is one third of the Rosary, either in honor of the five Joyful Mysteries, which are the Annunciation, the Visitation, the Nativity of Jesus Christ, the Purification, and the Finding of Our Lord in the Temple; or in honor of the five Sorrowful Mysteries, which are the Agony of Our Lord in the Garden of Olives, His Scourging, His Crowning with Thorns, His Carrying of the Cross, and His Crucifixion; or in honor of the five Glorious Mysteries, which are the Resurrection, the Ascension, the Descent of the Holy Ghost at Pentecost, the Assumption of our Blessed Lady, body and soul, into Heaven, and her Coronation by the Three Persons of the Most Holy Trinity. We may also say a chaplet of six or seven

decades in honor of the years which we believe Our
Lady lived on earth; or the Little Crown of the
Blessed Virgin, composed of three Our Fathers and
twelve Hail Marys, in honor of her crown of twelve
stars or privileges; or the Office of Our Lady, so
universally received and recited in the Church; or the
little Psalter of the holy Virgin, which St. Bonaventure composed in her honor, and which is so tender
and so devout that one cannot say it without being
moved by it; or fourteen Our Fathers and Hail Marys
in honor of her fourteen joys; or some other prayers,
hymns and canticles of the Church, such as the *Salve
Regina,* the *Alma,* the *Ave Regina Coelorum,* or the
Regina Coeli, according to the different seasons; or the
Ave Maris Stella, the *O Gloriosa Domina,* the *Magnificat,* or some other practices of devotion, of which
books are full; (7) to sing, or have sung, spiritual canticles in her honor; (8) to make a number of genuflec-
tions or reverences, while saying, for example, every
morning, sixty or a hundred times, *Ave Maria, Virgo
Fidelis ("Hail Mary, Faithful Virgin"),* to obtain from
God through her the grace to be faithful to the graces
of God during the day; and then again in the evening,
Ave Maria, Mater Misericordiae ("Hail Mary, Mother
of Mercy") to ask pardon of God through her for the
sins that we have committed during the day; (9) to
take care of her confraternities, to adorn her altars, to
crown and ornament her images; (10) to carry her images, or to have them carried, in procession, and to
carry a picture or an image of her about our own persons, as a mighty arm against the evil spirit; (11) to
have copies of her name or picture made and placed
in churches, or in houses, or on the gates and
entrances into cities, churches and houses; (12) to

consecrate ourselves to her in a special and solemn manner.

117. There are numerous other practices of true devotion toward the Blessed Virgin which the Holy Ghost has inspired in saintly souls and which are very sanctifying; they can be read at length in the *Paradise Opened to Philagius* of Father Barry, the Jesuit, in which he has collected a great number of devotions which the saints have practiced in honor of Our Lady—devotions which serve marvelously to sanctify our souls, provided they are performed as they ought to be, that is to say, (1) with a good and pure intention to please God only, to unite ourselves to Jesus Christ as to our Last End, and to edify our neighbor; (2) with attention and without voluntary distraction; (3) with devotion, equally avoiding precipitation and negligence; (4) with modesty, and a respectful and edifying posture of the body.

§ 2. Its *perfect* practice.

118. But after all, I loudly protest that, having read nearly all the books which profess to treat of devotion to Our Lady, and having conversed familiarly with the best and wisest of men of these latter times, I have never known nor heard of any practice of devotion toward her at all equal to the one which I now wish to unfold; demanding from the soul, as it does, more sacrifices for God, ridding the soul more of itself and of its self-love, keeping it more faithfully in grace and grace more faithfully in it, uniting it more perfectly and more easily to Jesus Christ; and finally, being more glorious to God, more sanctifying to the soul and more useful to our neighbor than any other of the

devotions to her.

119. As the essential of this devotion consists in the interior which it ought to form, it will not be equally understood by everybody. Some will stop at what is exterior in it, and will go no further, and these will be the greatest number. Some, in small number, will enter into its inward spirit; but they will only mount one step. Who will mount to the second step? Who will get as far as the third? Lastly, who will so advance as to make this devotion his habitual state? He alone to whom the spirit of Jesus Christ shall have revealed this secret, the faultlessly faithful soul whom He shall conduct there Himself, to advance from virtue to virtue, from grace to grace, from light to light, until he arrives at the transformation of himself into Jesus Christ, and to the plenitude of His age on earth and of His glory in Heaven.

NOTES

1. This description by St. Louis De Montfort is not exaggerated in the light of the activity of "critical devotees" at this period in spreading among the faithful such virulent writings as *Salutary Advice of the Blessed Virgin to Her Indiscreet Devotees*, by Widenfelt. Cf. Lhoumeau: *La vie Spirituelle à l'école de St. Louis Marie de Montfort*, p. 17; also Terrien, *La Mère de Dieu et la mère des hommes*, Vol. IV, p. 478.

2. In this context, "sensible" means "of the senses"; it refers to sweet feelings of religious fervor.

3. Because of its continual variations, the moon is often taken by ancient mystical writers as a symbol of the changing, inconstant soul. Cf. *Eccles.* 27:12; St. Bernard, *Sermo super signum magnum*, no. 3.

4. Notice the association of these two terms, "child" and "slave." Similar use of these terms was made by the *Catechism of the Council of Trent* (Part 1, Cap. 3, De secundo symboli articulo, in

fine).

5. The prediction was fulfilled to the letter. Throughout the whole eighteenth century, the spiritual sons of St. Louis De Montfort were persecuted by the Jansenists for their zeal in spreading this devotion; and the precious manuscript of De Montfort remained hidden during the troublous times of the French Revolution, and was brought to light only in the year 1842, when it was found in a chest of old books by a Montfort Father.

6. See no. 257-265.

— Part Two —

PERFECT DEVOTION TO THE BLESSED VIRGIN MARY

Nature

Motives

Wonderful Effects

Practices

Chapter I

NATURE OF PERFECT DEVOTION TO THE BLESSED VIRGIN
OR
PERFECT CONSECRATION TO JESUS CHRIST

120. All our perfection consists in being conformed, united and consecrated to Jesus Christ; and therefore the most perfect of all devotions is, without any doubt, that which the most perfectly conforms, unites and consecrates us to Jesus Christ. Now, Mary being the most conformed of all creatures to Jesus Christ, it follows that, of all devotions, that which most consecrates and conforms the soul to Our Lord is devotion to His holy Mother, and that the more a soul is consecrated to Mary, the more it is consecrated to Jesus.

Hence it comes to pass that the most perfect consecration to Jesus Christ is nothing else but a perfect and entire consecration of ourselves to the Blessed Virgin, and this is the devotion which I teach; or, in other words, a perfect renewal of the vows and promises of holy Baptism.

— Article One —
A PERFECT AND ENTIRE CONSECRATION
OF ONESELF TO THE BLESSED VIRGIN

121. This devotion consists, then, in giving ourselves entirely to Our Lady, in order to belong entirely

77

to Jesus through her.[1] We must give her (1) our body,
with all its senses and its members; (2) our soul, with
all its powers; (3) our exterior goods of fortune,
whether present or to come; (4) our interior and
spiritual goods, which are our merits and our virtues,
and our good works, past, present and future. In a
word, we must give her all we have in the order of
nature and in the order of grace, and all that may
become ours in the future, in the orders of nature,
grace and glory; and this we must do without the
reserve of so much as one farthing, one hair, or one
least good action; and we must do it also for all eternity; and we must do it, further, without pretending to,
or hoping for, any other recompense for our offering
and service except the honor of belonging to Jesus
Christ through Mary and in Mary—as though that
sweet Mistress were not (as she always *is*) the most
generous and the most grateful of creatures.

122. Here we must note that there are two things in
the good works we perform, namely, satisfaction and
merit; in other words, their satisfactory or impetratory
value, and their meritorious value. The satisfactory or
impetratory value of a good action is that action inasmuch as it satisfies for the pain due to sin, or obtains some new grace; the meritorious value, or the
merit, is the good action inasmuch as it merits grace
now and eternal glory hereafter. Now, in this consecration of ourselves to Our Lady, we give her all the
satisfactory, impetratory and meritorious value of our
actions; in other words, the satisfactions and the
merits of all our good works. We give her all our
merits, graces and virtues—not to communicate them
to others, for our merits, graces and virtues are, properly speaking, incommunicable, and it is only Jesus

Christ who, in making Himself our surety with His Father, is able to communicate His merits—but we give her them to keep them, augment them and embellish them for us, as we shall explain by and by.[2] Our satisfactions, however, we give her to communicate to whom she likes, and for the greatest glory of God.

123. It follows from this that:

§ 1. By this devotion we give to Jesus Christ in the most perfect manner, inasmuch as it is by Mary's hands, all we can give Him, and far more than by any other devotions in which we give Him either a part of our time, or a part of our good works, or a part of our satisfactions and mortifications; because here everything is given and consecrated to Him, even the right of disposing of our interior goods and of the satisfactions which we gain by our good works day after day. This is more than we do even in a religious order. In religious orders we give God the goods of fortune by the vow of poverty, the goods of the body by the vow of chastity, our own will by the vow of obedience, and sometimes the liberty of the body by the vow of cloister. But we do not by these vows give Him the liberty or the right to dispose of the value of our good works; and we do not strip ourselves, as far as a Christian man can do so, of that which is dearest and most precious, namely, our merits and our satisfactions.

124. § 2. A person who is thus voluntarily consecrated and sacrificed to Jesus Christ through Mary can no longer dispose of the value of any of his good actions. All he suffers, all he thinks, all the good he says or does, belongs to Mary, in order that she may dispose of it according to the will of her Son and His

greatest glory—without, however, that dependence interfering in any way with the obligations of the state we may be in at present or may be placed in for the future; for example, without interfering with the obligations of a priest who, by his office or otherwise, ought to apply the satisfactory and impetratory value of the Holy Mass to some private person. For we make the offering of this devotion only according to the order of God and the duties of our state.

125. § 3. We consecrate ourselves at one and the same time to the most holy Virgin and to Jesus Christ; to the most holy Virgin as to the perfect means which Jesus Christ has chosen whereby to unite Himself to us, and us to Him; and to Our Lord as to our Last End, to whom, as our Redeemer and our God, we owe all we are.

— Article Two —
A PERFECT RENEWAL OF THE VOWS OF HOLY BAPTISM

126. I have said[3] that this devotion may rightly be called a perfect renewal of the vows or promises of holy Baptism.

For every Christian, before his Baptism, was the slave of the devil, seeing that he belonged to him. He has in his Baptism, by his own mouth or by his sponsor's, solemnly renounced Satan, his pomps and his works; and he has taken Jesus Christ for his Master and Sovereign Lord, to depend upon Him in the quality of a slave of love. That is what we do by the present devotion. We renounce, as is expressed in the formula of consecration,[4] the devil, the world, sin and self; and we give ourselves entirely to Jesus Christ by the hands of Mary. Nay, we even do something more; for in Baptism, we ordinarily speak by the mouth of another, our godfather or godmother, and so we give ourselves to Jesus Christ not by ourselves but through another. But in this devotion we do it by ourselves, voluntarily, knowing what we are doing.

Moreover, in holy Baptism we do not give ourselves to Jesus by the hands of Mary, at least not in an explicit manner; and we do not give Him the value of our good actions. We remain entirely free after Baptism, either to apply them to whom we please or to keep them for ourselves. But by this devotion we give ourselves to Our Lord explicitly by the hands of Mary, and we consecrate to Him the value of all our actions.

127. Men, says St. Thomas, make a vow at their Baptism to renounce the devil and all his pomps.[5] This vow, says St. Augustine, is the greatest and most indispensable of all vows.[6] It is thus also that canonists speak: "The principal vow is the one we make at Baptism." Yet who has kept this great vow? Who is it that faithfully performs the promises of holy Baptism? Have not almost all Christians swerved from the loyalty which they promised Jesus in their Baptism? Whence can come this universal disobedience, except from our forgetfulness of the promises and obligations of holy Baptism, and from the fact that hardly anyone ratifies, of himself, the contract he made with God by those who stood sponsors for him?

128. This is so true that the Council of Sens, convoked by order of Louis the Debonair to remedy the disorders of Christians, which were then so great, judged that the principal cause of that corruption of morals arose from the oblivion and the ignorance in

which men lived of the obligations of holy Baptism; and it could think of no better means for remedying so great an evil than to persuade Christians to renew the vows and promises of Baptism.

129. The *Catechism of the Council of Trent,* the faithful interpreter of that holy Council, exhorts the parish priests to do the same thing, and to induce the people to remind themselves, and to believe, that they are bound and consecrated as slaves to Our Lord Jesus Christ, their Redeemer and their Lord. These are its words: "The parish priest shall exhort the faithful people so that they may know that it is most just ... that we should devote and consecrate ourselves forever to our Redeemer and Lord as His very slaves."[7]

130. Now, if the Councils, the Fathers and even experience show us that the best means of remedying the irregularities of Christians is by making them call to mind the obligations of their Baptism, and persuading them to renew now the vows they made then, is it not only right that we should do it in a perfect manner, by this devotion and consecration of ourselves to Our Lord through His holy Mother? I say "in a perfect manner," because in thus consecrating ourselves to Him, we make use of the most perfect of all means, namely, the Blessed Virgin.

OBJECTIONS AND ANSWERS

131. No one can object to this devotion as being either a new or an indifferent one. It is not new, because the Councils, the Fathers and many authors both ancient and modern speak of this consecration to Our Lord, or renewal of the vows and promises of

Baptism, as of a thing anciently practiced, and which they counsel to all Christians. Neither is it a matter of indifference, because the principal source of all disorders, and consequently of the eternal perdition of Christians, comes from their forgetfulness and indifference about this practice.

132. But some may object that this devotion, in making us give to Our Lord, by Our Lady's hands, the value of all our good works, prayers, mortifications and alms, puts us in a state of incapacity for assisting the souls of our parents, friends and benefactors.

I answer them as follows:

§ 1. That it is not credible that our parents, friends and benefactors should suffer from the fact of our being devoted and consecrated without exception to the service of Our Lord and His holy Mother. To think this would be to think unworthily of the goodness and power of Jesus and Mary, who know well how to assist our parents, friends and benefactors, out of our own little spiritual revenue or by other ways.

§ 2. This practice does not hinder us from praying for others, whether dead or living, although the application of our good works depends on the will of our Blessed Lady. On the contrary, it is this very thing which will lead us to pray with more confidence; just as a rich person who has given all his wealth to his prince in order to honor him the more, would beg the prince all the more confidently to give an alms to one of his friends who should ask for it. It would even be a source of pleasure to the prince to be given an occasion of proving his gratitude toward a person who had stripped himself to clothe him, and impoverished himself to honor him. We must say the same of our

Blessed Lord and of Our Lady. They will never let themselves be outdone in gratitude.

133. Someone may perhaps say, "If I give to our Blessed Lady all the value of my actions to apply to whom she wills, I may have to suffer a long time in Purgatory."

This objection, which comes from self-love and ignorance of the generosity of God and His holy Mother, refutes itself. A fervent and generous soul who gives God all he has, without reserve, so that he can do nothing more; who lives only for the glory and reign of Jesus Christ, through His holy Mother, and who makes an entire sacrifice of himself to bring it about—will this generous and liberal soul, I say, be more punished in the other world because it has been more liberal and more disinterested than others? Far, indeed, will that be from the truth! Rather, it is toward that soul, as we shall see by what follows, that Our Lord and His holy Mother are the most liberal in this world and in the other, in the orders of nature, grace and glory.

134. But we must now, as briefly as we can, run over the motives which ought to recommend this devotion to us, the marvelous effects it produces in the souls of the faithful, and its practices.

NOTES

1. St. John Damascene: *"Mentem, animam, corpus, nos ipsosque totos tibi consecramus." (Sermo I in Dormitione B.V.).*
2. Cf no. 146 and following.
3. Cf. no. 120.
4. The consecration is to be found on page 196.
5. *Summa Theologica,* IIa IIae, Q. 88, art. 2, ad 1.
6. *Epistola 59 ad Paulinum.*

7. *Catech. Conc. Trid.* (Parte Ia, caput 3, art. 2, no. 15, De secundo
   Symboli articulo, in fine).

Chapter II

MOTIVES OF THIS PERFECT CONSECRATION

— First Motive —
IT DEVOTES US ENTIRELY
TO THE SERVICE OF GOD

135. *The first motive, which shows us the excellence of this consecration of ourselves to Jesus Christ by the hands of Mary.*

If we can conceive on earth no employment more lofty than the service of God—if the least servant of God is richer, more powerful and more noble than all the kings and emperors of this earth, unless they also are the servants of God—what must be the riches, the power and the dignity of the faithful and perfect servant of God, who is devoted to His service entirely and without reserve, to the utmost extent possible? Such is the faithful and loving slave of Jesus in Mary who has given himself up entirely to the service of that King of Kings, by the hands of His holy Mother, and has reserved nothing for himself. Not all the gold of earth nor all the beauties of the heavens can repay him.

136. The other congregations, associations and confraternities erected in honor of Our Lord and His holy Mother, which do such immense good in Christendom, do not make us give everything without reserve. They prescribe to their members only certain

practices and actions to satisfy their obligations. They leave them free for all other actions and moments and occupations. But this devotion makes us give to Jesus and Mary, without reserve, all our thoughts, words, actions and sufferings, every moment of our life, in such wise that whether we wake or sleep, whether we eat or drink, whether we do great actions or very little ones, it is always true to say that whatever we do, even without thinking of it, is, by virtue of our offering—at least if it has not been intentionally retracted—done for Jesus and Mary. What a consolation this is!

137. Moreover, as I have already said,[1] there is no other practice equal to this for enabling us to rid ourselves easily of a certain proprietorship which imperceptibly creeps into our best actions. Our good Jesus gives us this great grace in recompense for the heroic and disinterested action of giving over to Him, by the hands of His holy Mother, all the value of our good works. If He gives a hundredfold even in this world to those who, for His love, quit outward and temporal and perishable goods (*Matt.* 19:29), what will that hundredfold be which He will give to the man who sacrifices for Him even his inward and spiritual goods!

138. Jesus, our great Friend, has given Himself to us without reserve, body and soul, virtues, graces and merits. "He has bought the whole of me with the whole of Himself," says St. Bernard. Is it not then a simple matter of justice and of gratitude that we should give Him all that we can give Him? He has been the first to be liberal toward us; let us, at least, be the second; and then, in life and death and throughout all eternity, we shall find Him still more

liberal. "With the liberal He will be liberal."

— Second Motive —
IT MAKES US IMITATE THE EXAMPLE
OF JESUS CHRIST AND OF THE HOLY TRINITY
AND PRACTICE HUMILITY

139. *The second motive, which shows us how just it is in itself, and how advantageous to Christians, to consecrate themselves entirely to the Blessed Virgin by this practice, in order to belong more perfectly to Jesus Christ.*

This good Master did not disdain to shut Himself up in the womb of the Blessed Virgin, as a captive and as a loving slave, and later to be subject and obedient to her for thirty years. It is here, I repeat, that the human mind loses itself, when it seriously reflects on the conduct of the Incarnate Wisdom who willed to give Himself to men—not directly, though He might have done so, but through the Blessed Virgin. He did not will to come into the world at the age of a perfect man, independent of others, but like a poor little babe, dependent on the care and support of this holy Mother. He is that Infinite Wisdom who had a boundless desire to glorify God His Father and to save men; and yet He found no more perfect means, no shorter way to do it, than to submit Himself in all things to the Blessed Virgin, not only during the first eight, ten or fifteen years of His life, like other children, but for thirty years! He gave more glory to God His Father during all that time of submission to and dependence on our Blessed Lady than He would have given Him if He had employed those thirty years in working miracles, in preaching to the whole world and in converting all men—all of which He would have done, could He have thereby contributed more to God's glory. Oh, how highly we glorify God when, after the example of Jesus, we submit ourselves to Mary!

Having, then, before our eyes an example so plain and so well known to the whole world, are we so senseless as to imagine that we can find a more perfect or a shorter means of glorifying God than that of submitting ourselves to Mary, after the example of her Son?

140. Let us recall here, as a proof of the dependence we ought to have on our Blessed Lady, what I have said above[2] in bringing forward the example which the Father, the Son and the Holy Ghost give of this dependence. The Father has not given, and does not give, His Son, except by her; He has no children but by her, and communicates no graces but through her. The Son has not been formed for the whole world in general, except by her; and He is not daily formed and engendered except by her, in union with the Holy Ghost; neither does He communicate His merits and His virtues except through her. The Holy Ghost has not formed Jesus Christ except by her; neither does He form the members of Our Lord's Mystical Body, except by her; and through her alone does He dispense His favors and His gifts. After so many and such pressing examples of the Most Holy Trinity, can we without extreme blindness dispense with Mary, can we fail to consecrate ourselves to her and depend on her for the purpose of going to God and sacrificing ourselves to God?

141. Here are some passages of the Fathers which I have chosen to prove what has just been said:

"Mary has two sons, a God-Man and a pure man;

she is Mother of the first corporally, of the second spiritually."[3]

"This is the will of God, who wished us to have all things through Mary; if, therefore, there is in us any hope, any grace, any salutary gift, we know it comes to us through her."[4]

"All the gifts, virtues and graces of the Holy Ghost are distributed by Mary, to whom she wishes, when she wishes, the way she wishes and as much as she wishes."[5]

"Since you were unworthy to receive the divine graces, they were given to Mary, so that whatever you would have, you would receive through her."[6]

142. God, says St. Bernard, seeing that we are unworthy to receive His graces immediately from His own hand, gives them to Mary, in order that we may have through her whatever He wills to give us; and He also finds His glory in receiving, through the hands of Mary, the gratitude, respect and love which we owe Him for His benefits. It is most just, then, that we imitate this conduct of God, in order, as the same St. Bernard says,[7] that grace return to its Author by the same channel through which it came: "That grace should return to the giver by the same channel through which it came."

This is precisely what our devotion does. We offer and consecrate all we are and all we have to the Blessed Virgin in order that Our Lord may receive through her mediation the glory and the gratitude which we owe Him. We acknowledge ourselves unworthy and unfit to approach His Infinite Majesty by ourselves; and it is on this account that we avail ourselves of the intercession of the most holy Virgin.

143. Moreover, this devotion is a practice of great

humility, which God loves above all the other virtues. A soul which exalts itself abases God; a soul which abases itself exalts God. God resists the proud and gives His grace to the humble.[8] If you abase yourself, thinking yourself unworthy to appear before Him and to draw nigh to Him, He descends and lowers Himself to come to you, to take pleasure in you and to exalt you in spite of yourself. On the contrary, when you are bold enough to approach God without a mediator, God flies from you and you cannot reach Him. Oh, how He loves humility of heart! It is to this humility that this devotion induces us, because it teaches us never to draw nigh, of ourselves, to Our Lord, however sweet and merciful He may be, but always to avail ourselves of the intercession of our Blessed Lady, whether it be to appear before God, or to speak to Him, or to draw near to Him, or to offer Him anything, or to unite and consecrate ourselves to Him.

— Third Motive —
IT OBTAINS FOR US THE GOOD OFFICES OF THE BLESSED VIRGIN

I. Mary Gives Herself to Her Slave of Love

144. The most holy Virgin, who is a Mother of sweetness and mercy, and who never lets herself be outdone in love and liberality, seeing that we give ourselves entirely to her, to honor and to serve her, and for that end strip ourselves of all that is dearest to us, in order to adorn her, meets us in the same spirit. She also gives her whole self, and gives it in an unspeakable manner, to him who gives all to her. She causes him to be engulfed in the abyss of her graces.

She adorns him with her merits; she supports him with her power; she illuminates him with her light; she inflames him with her love; she communicates to him her virtues: her humility, her faith, her purity and the rest. She makes herself his bail, his supplement, and his dear all toward Jesus. In a word, as that consecrated person is all Mary's, so Mary is all his, after such a fashion that we can say of that perfect servant and child[9] of Mary what St. John the Evangelist said of himself, that he took the holy Virgin for his own: "The disciple took her for his own." (*Jn*. 19:27).

145. It is this which produces in the soul, if it is faithful, a great distrust, contempt and hatred of self, and a great confidence in and self-abandonment to the Blessed Virgin, its good Mistress. A man no longer, as before, relies on his own dispositions, intentions, merits, virtues and good works; because, having made an entire sacrifice of them to Jesus Christ by that good Mother, he has but one treasure now, where all his goods are laid up, and that is no longer in himself, for his treasure is Mary.

This is what makes him approach Our Lord without servile or scrupulous fear, and pray to Him with great confidence. This is what makes him share the sentiments of the devout and learned Abbot Rupert, who, alluding to the victory that Jacob gained over the angel (*Gen*. 32:24), said to our Blessed Lady these beautiful words: "O Mary, my Princess, Immaculate Mother of the God-Man, Jesus Christ, I desire to wrestle with that man, namely, the Divine Word, not armed with my own merits but with yours."[10]

Oh, how strong and mighty we are with Jesus Christ when we are armed with the merits and intercession of the worthy Mother of God, who, as St. Augustine says, has lovingly vanquished the Most High.

II. *Mary Purifies Our Good Works, Embellishes Them and Makes Them Acceptable to Her Son*

146. As by this practice we give to Our Lord, by His Mother's hands, all our good works, that good Mother purifies them, embellishes them and makes them acceptable to her Son.

§ 1. She purifies them of all the stain of self-love, and of that imperceptible attachment to created things which slips unnoticed into our best actions. As soon as they are in her most pure and fruitful hands, those same hands, which have never been sullied or idle and which purify whatever they touch, take away from the present which we give her all that was spoiled or imperfect about it.

147. § 2. She embellishes our works, adorning them with her own merits and virtues. It is as if a peasant, wishing to gain the friendship and benevolence of the king, went to the queen and presented her with a fruit which was his whole revenue, in order that she might present it to the king. The queen, having accepted the poor little offering from the peasant, would place the fruit on a large and beautiful dish of gold, and so, on the peasant's behalf, would present it to the king. Then the fruit, however unworthy in itself to be a king's present, would become worthy of his majesty because of the dish of gold on which it rested and the person who presented it.

148. § 3. She presents these good works to Jesus Christ; for she keeps nothing of what is given her for herself, as if she were our last end. She faithfully passes it all on to Jesus. If we give to her, we give

necessarily to Jesus. If we praise her or glorify her, she immediately praises and glorifies Jesus. As of old when St. Elizabeth praised her, so now when we praise her and bless her, she sings: "My soul doth magnify the Lord." (*Lk.* 1:46).

149. She persuades Jesus to accept these good works, however little and poor the present may be for that Saint of Saints and that King of Kings. When we present anything to Jesus by ourselves, and relying on our own efforts and dispositions, Jesus examines the offering, and often rejects it because of the stains it has contracted through self-love, just as of old He rejected the sacrifices of the Jews when they were full of their own will. But when we present Him anything by the pure and virginal hands of His well-beloved, we take Him by His weak side, if it is allowable to use such a term. He does not consider so much the thing that is given Him as the Mother who presents it. He does not consider so much whence the offering comes, as by whom it comes. Thus Mary, who is never repelled but always well received by her Son, makes everything she presents to Him, great or small, acceptable to His Majesty. Mary has but to present it for Jesus to accept it and be pleased with it. St. Bernard used to give to those whom he conducted to perfection this great counsel: "When you want to offer anything to God, take care to offer it by the most agreeable and worthy hands of Mary, unless you wish to have it rejected."[11]

150. Is not this what nature itself suggests to the little with regard to the great, as we have already seen?[12] Why should not grace lead us to do the same thing with regard to God, who is infinitely exalted above us and before whom we are less than atoms—

especially since we have an advocate so powerful that she is never refused; so ingenious that she knows all the secret ways of winning the heart of God; and so good and charitable that she repels no one, however little and wretched he may be.

I shall speak further on[13] of the true figure of these truths in the story of Jacob and Rebecca.

— Fourth Motive —
IT IS AN EXCELLENT MEANS OF PROCURING GOD'S GREATER GLORY

151. This devotion, faithfully practiced, is an excellent means of making sure that the value of all our good works shall be employed for the greater glory of God. Scarcely anyone acts for that noble end, although we are all under an obligation to do so. Either we do not know where the greater glory of God is to be found, or we do not wish to find it. But our Blessed Lady, to whom we cede the value and merit of our good works, knows most perfectly where the greater glory of God is to be found; and inasmuch as she never does anything except for the greater glory of God, a perfect servant of that good Mistress, who is wholly consecrated to her, may say with the hardiest assurance that the value of all his actions, thoughts and words is employed for the greater glory of God, unless he purposely revokes his offering. Is there any consolation equal to this for a soul who loves God with a pure and disinterested love, and who prizes the glory and interest of God far beyond his own?

— Fifth Motive —
IT LEADS US TO UNION
WITH OUR LORD

152. This devotion is an *easy, short, perfect* and *secure* way of attaining union with Our Lord, in which union the perfection of a Christian consists.

I. It Is an Easy Way

It is an easy way. It is the way which Jesus Christ Himself trod in coming to us, and in which there is no obstacle in reaching Him. It is true that we can attain divine union by other roads; but it is by many more crosses and strange deaths, and with many more difficulties, which we shall find it hard to overcome. We must pass through obscure nights, through combats, through strange agonies, over craggy mountains, through cruel thorns and over frightful deserts. But by the path of Mary we pass more gently and more tranquilly.

We do find, it is true, great battles to fight, and great hardships to master; but that good Mother makes herself so present and so near to her faithful servants, to enlighten them in their darknesses and their doubts, to strengthen them in their fears, and to sustain them in their struggles and their difficulties, that in truth this virginal path to find Jesus Christ is a path of roses and honey compared with the other paths. There have been some saints, but they have been in small numbers, who have walked upon this sweet path to go to Jesus, because the Holy Ghost, faithful Spouse of Mary, by a singular grace disclosed it to them. Such were St. Ephrem, St. John

Damascene, St. Bernard, St. Bernardine, St. Bonaventure, St. Francis de Sales, and others. But the rest of the saints, who are the greater number, although they have all had devotion to our Blessed Lady, nevertheless have either not at all, or at least very little, entered upon this way. That is why they have had to pass through ruder and more dangerous trials.

153. How is it, then, some of the faithful servants of Mary will say to me, that the faithful servants of this good Mother have so many occasions of suffering, nay, even more than others who are not so devout to her? They are contradicted, they are persecuted, they are calumniated, the world cannot endure them;[14] or again, they walk in interior darkness and in deserts where there is not the least drop of the dew of Heaven. If this devotion to our Blessed Lady makes the road to Jesus easier, how is it that they who follow it are the most despised of men?

154. I reply that it is quite true that the most faithful servants of the Blessed Virgin, being also her greatest favorites, receive from her the greatest graces and favors of Heaven, which are crosses. But I maintain that it is also the servants of Mary who carry these crosses with more ease, more merit and more glory. That which would stay the progress of another a thousand times over, or perhaps would make him fall, does not once stop their steps, but rather enables them to advance; because that good Mother, all full of grace and of the unction of the Holy Ghost, prepares her servants' crosses with so much maternal sweetness and pure love as to make them gladly acceptable, no matter how bitter they may be in themselves; and I believe that a person who wishes to be devout, and to live piously in Jesus Christ, and consequently to suffer

persecutions and carry his cross daily, either will never carry great crosses, or will not carry them joyously or perseveringly, without a tender devotion to Our Lady, which is the sweetmeat and confection of crosses; just as a person would not be able to eat unripe fruits without a great effort which he could hardly keep up, unless they had been preserved in sugar.

II. It Is a Short Way

155. This devotion to our Blessed Lady is a short road[15] to find Jesus Christ, both because it is a road from which we do not stray, and because, as I have just said, it is a road we tread with joy and facility, and consequently with promptitude. We make more progress in a brief period of submission to and dependence on Mary than in whole years of following our own will and of relying upon ourselves. A man obedient and submissive to Mary shall sing the signal victories which he shall gain over his enemies. (*Prov.* 21:28). They will try to hinder his advancing, or to make him retrace his steps or fall; this is true. But with the support, the aid and the guidance of Mary, he shall advance with giant strides toward Jesus, without falling, without drawing back one step, without even slackening his pace, along the same path by which he knows (*Ps.* 18:6) that Jesus also came to us with giant strides and in the briefest space of time.

156. Why do you think that Jesus lived so few years on earth, and of those few years, spent nearly all of them in subjection and obedience to His Mother? The truth is that, being perfected in a short time (*Wis.* 4:13), He lived a long time—longer than Adam,

whose fall He had come to repair, although the patriarch lived above nine hundred years. Jesus Christ lived a long time because He lived in complete subjection to His holy Mother, and closely united with her, in order that He might thus obey His Father. For (1) the Holy Ghost says that a man who honors his mother is like a man who layeth up a treasure; that is to say, he who honors Mary, his Mother, to the extent of subjecting himself to her and obeying her in all things, will soon become exceedingly rich, because he is every day amassing treasures by the secret of that touchstone: "He who honors his mother is as one who lays up a treasure" (*Ecclus.* 3:5); (2) because, according to a mystical interpretation of the inspired text, "My old age is to be found in the mercy of the bosom" (*Ps.* 91:11), it is in the bosom of Mary, which has surrounded and engendered a perfect man (*Jer.* 31:22), and has had the capacity of containing Him whom the whole universe could neither contain nor comprehend[16]—it is, I say, in the bosom of Mary that they who are youthful become elders in light, in holiness, in experience and in wisdom, and that we arrive in a few years at the fullness of the age of Jesus Christ.

III. It Is a Perfect Way

157. This practice of devotion to our Blessed Lady is also a perfect path by which to go and unite ourselves to Jesus; because the divine Mary is the most perfect and the most holy of creatures, and because Jesus, who has come to us most perfectly, took no other road for His great and admirable journey. The Most High, the Incomprehensible, the Inaccessible,

He Who is, has willed to come to us, little worms of earth who are nothing. How has He done this? The Most High has come down to us perfectly and divinely, by the humble Mary, without losing anything of His divinity and sanctity. So it is by Mary that the very little ones are to ascend perfectly and divinely, without any fear, to the Most High. The Incomprehensible has allowed Himself to be comprehended and perfectly contained by the little Mary, without losing anything of His immensity. So also it is by the little Mary that we must let ourselves be contained and guided perfectly without any reserve. The Inaccessible has drawn near to us and has united Himself closely, perfectly and even personally to our humanity, by Mary, without losing anything of His majesty. So also it is by Mary that we must draw near to God and unite ourselves perfectly and closely to His Majesty without fear of being repulsed. In a word, He Who is has willed to come to that which is not, and to make that which is not, become He Who is; and He has done this perfectly in giving Himself and subjecting Himself entirely to the young Virgin Mary, without ceasing to be in time He who is from all eternity. In like manner, it is by Mary that we, who are nothing, can become like to God by grace and glory, by giving ourselves to her so perfectly and entirely as to be nothing in ourselves, but everything in her, without fear of delusion.

158. Make for me, if you will, a new road to go to Jesus, and pave it with all the merits of the blessed, adorn it with all their heroic virtues, illuminate and embellish it with all the lights and beauties of the angels, and let all the angels and saints be there themselves, to escort, defend and sustain those who are

ready to walk there; and yet in truth, in simple truth, I say boldly, and I repeat that I say truly, I would prefer to this new, perfect path the immaculate way of Mary. "He made my way blameless." (*Ps.* 17:33). It is the way without stain or spot, without original or actual sin, without shadow or darkness. When my sweet Jesus comes a second time on earth in His glory, as it is most certain He will do, to reign there, He will choose no other way for His journey than the divine Mary, by whom He came the first time so surely and so perfectly. But there will be a difference between His first and His last coming. The first time He came secretly and hiddenly; the second time He will come gloriously and resplendently. But both times He will have come perfectly, because both times He will have come by Mary. Alas! Here is a mystery which is not understood. "Here let all tongues be mute."

IV. *It Is a Secure Way*

159. This devotion to our Blessed Lady is also a secure way to go to Jesus and to acquire perfection by uniting ourselves to Him.

§ 1. It is a secure way, because the practice which I am teaching is not new. Father Boudon,[17] who died a short time ago in the odor of sanctity, says in a book which he composed on this devotion that it is so ancient that we cannot fix precisely the date of its beginning. It is, however, certain that for more than seven hundred years we find traces of it in the Church.[18]

St. Odilon, the Abbot of Cluny, who lived about the year 1040, was one of the first who publicly practiced it in France, as is told in his life.

Peter Cardinal Damian[19] relates that in the year

1016 Blessed Marino, his brother, made himself a slave of the Blessed Virgin in the presence of his director in a most edifying manner. He put a rope around his neck, took the discipline, and laid on the altar a sum of money, as a token of his devotedness and consecration to Our Lady; and he continued this devotion so faithfully during his whole life that he deserved to be visited and consoled at his death by his good Mistress, and to receive from her mouth the promise of paradise in recompense for his services.[20]

Caesarius Bollandus[21] mentions an illustrious knight, Vautier de Birbac, a near relative of the Duke of Louvain, who about the year 1300 consecrated himself to the Blessed Virgin.[22]

This devotion was also practiced by several private individuals up to the seventeenth century, when it became public.

160. Father Simon de Roias, of the Order of the Most Holy Trinity, known as the Order of Redemption of Captives, and preacher of Philip III, made this devotion popular in Spain[23] and Germany;[24] and at the request of Philip III, obtained of Gregory XV ample indulgences for those who practiced it.

Father de Los Rios, the Augustinian, devoted himself, with his intimate friend, Father de Roias, to spreading this devotion throughout Spain and Germany both by preaching and by writing.[25] He composed a thick volume called *Hierarchia Mariana,*[26] in which he treats with as much piety as learning of the antiquity, excellence and solidity of this devotion.[27]

161. In the seventeenth century the Theatine Fathers established this devotion in Italy, Sicily and Savoy.

Father Stanislaus Phalacius, the Jesuit, furthered

this devotion wonderfully in Poland.[28]

Father de Los Rios, in his work just cited, quotes the names of princes, princesses, bishops and cardinals of different kingdoms, who embraced this devotion.

Cornelius à Lapide, as praiseworthy for his piety as for his profound erudition, having been commissioned by several bishops and theologians to examine this devotion, did so with great thoroughness and deliberation, and praised it in a manner which we might have expected from his well-known piety; and many other distinguished persons have followed his example.

The Jesuit Fathers, always zealous in the service of our Blessed Lady, in the name of the Sodalists of Cologne presented a little treatise[29] on this devotion to Duke Ferdinand of Bavaria, who was then Archbishop of Cologne. He approved it, granted permission for its printing, and exhorted all the parish priests and religious of his diocese to promote this solid devotion as much as they could.

162. Cardinal de Berulle, whose memory is held in veneration throughout all France, was one of the most zealous in spreading this devotion in that country, in spite of all the calumnies and persecutions which he suffered from critics and freethinkers. They accused him of novelty and superstition. They wrote and published a libel against him, in order to defame him; and they, or rather the devil by their ministry, made use of a thousand artifices to hinder his spreading the devotion in France. But that great and holy man only answered their calumnies by his patience; and he met the objections contained in their libel by a short treatise in which he most convincingly refuted them. He showed them that the devotion was founded on the

example of Jesus Christ, on the obligations which we have toward Him, and on the vows which we have made in holy Baptism. It was chiefly by means of this last reason that he shut his adversaries' mouths, making them see that this consecration to the holy Virgin, and to Jesus Christ by her hands, is nothing else than a perfect renewal of the vows and promises of Baptism. He has said many beautiful things about this practice, which can be read in his works.

163. We may also see in Father Boudon's book[30] the different Popes who have approved this devotion, the theologians who have examined it, the persecutions it has undergone and has overcome, and the thousands of persons who have embraced it, without any Pope ever having condemned it. Indeed, we cannot see how it could be condemned without overturning the foundations of Christianity.

It is clear, then, that this devotion is not new; and that if it is not common, that is because it is too precious to be relished and practiced by everyone.[31]

164. § 2. This devotion is a secure means of going to Jesus Christ, because it is the very characteristic of our Blessed Lady to conduct us surely to Jesus, just as it is the very characteristic of Jesus to conduct us surely to the Eternal Father. Spiritual persons, therefore, must not fall into the false belief that Mary can be a hindrance to them in attaining divine union; for is it possible that she who has found grace before God for the whole world in general and for each one in particular, should be a hindrance to a soul in finding the great grace of union with Him? Can it be possible that she who has been full and superabounding with graces, so united and transformed into God that it has been a kind of necessity that He should be

incarnate in her, should be a stumbling-block in the way of a soul's perfect union with God?

It is quite true that the view of other creatures, however holy, may perhaps at certain times retard divine union. But this cannot be said of Mary, as I have remarked before and shall never weary of repeating. One reason why so few souls come to the fullness of the age of Jesus Christ is that Mary, who is as much as ever the Mother of the Son, and as much as ever the fruitful spouse of the Holy Ghost, is not sufficiently formed in their hearts. He who wishes to have the fruit well ripened and well formed must have the tree that produces it; he who wishes to have the fruit of life, Jesus Christ, must have the tree of life, which is Mary; he who wishes to have in himself the operation of the Holy Ghost must have His faithful and inseparable spouse, the divine Mary, who makes Him fertile and fruit-bearing, as we have said elsewhere.[32]

165. Be persuaded, then, that the more you look at Mary in your prayers, contemplations, actions and sufferings, if not with a distinct and definite view, at least with a general and imperceptible one, the more perfectly will you find Jesus Christ, who is always, with Mary, great, powerful, active and incomprehensible—more than in Heaven or in any other creature. Thus, so far from the divine Mary, all absorbed in God, being an obstacle to the perfect in attaining union with God, there has never been up to this time, and there never will be, any creature who will aid us more efficaciously in this great work; either by the graces she will communicate to us for this purpose—for, as a saint has said, "No one can be filled with the thought of God except by her"[33]—or by the protection

she will afford us against the illusions and trickeries of the evil spirit.

166. Where Mary is, there the evil spirit is not. One of the most infallible marks we can have of our being conducted by the good spirit is our being very devout to Mary, thinking often of her and speaking often of her. This last is the thought of a saint,[34] who adds that as respiration is a certain sign the body is not dead, the frequent thought and loving invocation of Mary is a certain sign the soul is not dead by sin.

167. As it is Mary alone, says the Church (and the Holy Ghost who guides the Church), who makes all heresies come to naught—"Thou alone hast destroyed all heresies in the whole world"[35]—we may be sure that, however critics may grumble, no faithful client of Mary will ever fall into heresy or illusions, at least formal ones. He may very well err materially, take falsehood for truth, and the evil spirit for the good; and yet he will do even this less readily than others. But sooner or later he will acknowledge his material fault and error; and when he knows it, he will not be in any way self-opinionated by continuing to believe and maintain what he had once thought true.

168. Whoever, then, wishes to put aside the fear of illusion, which is the besetting timidity of men of prayer, and to advance in the way of perfection and surely and perfectly find Jesus Christ, let him embrace with great-heartedness—"with a great heart and willing mind" (*2 Mach.* 1:3)—this devotion to our Blessed Lady which perhaps he has not known before; let him enter into this excellent way which was unknown to him and which I now point out: "I show you a more excellent way." (*1 Cor.* 12:31). It is a path trodden by Jesus Christ, the Incarnate Wisdom, our sole Head.

One of His members cannot make a mistake in passing by the same road.

It is an easy road, because of the fullness of the grace and unction of the Holy Ghost which fills it to overflowing. No one wearies there; no one walking there ever has to retrace his steps. It is a short road which leads us to Jesus in a little time. It is a perfect road, where there is no mud, no dust, not the least spot of sin. Lastly, it is a secure road, which conducts us to Jesus Christ and life eternal in a straight and secure manner, without turning to the right hand or to the left. Let us, then, set forth upon that road and walk there day and night, until we come to the fullness of the age of Jesus Christ. (*Eph.* 4:13).

— Sixth Motive —
IT GIVES US GREAT INTERIOR LIBERTY

169. This practice of devotion gives to those who make use of it faithfully a great interior liberty, which is the liberty of the children of God. (*Rom.* 8:21). Since, by this devotion, we make ourselves slaves of Jesus Christ and consecrate ourselves entirely to Him in this capacity, our good Master, in recompense for the loving captivity in which we put ourselves, (1) takes from the soul all scruple and servile fear, which are capable only of cramping, imprisoning or confusing it; (2) He enlarges the heart with firm confidence in God, making it look upon Him as a Father; and (3) He inspires us with a tender and filial love.

170. Without stopping to prove these truths with arguments, I shall be content to relate here what I have read in the life of Mother Agnes of Jesus, a Dominican nun of the convent of Langeac, in

Auvergne, who died there in the odor of sanctity in
the year 1634. When she was only seven years old,
and was suffering from great spiritual anguish, she
heard a voice which told her that if she wished to be
delivered from her anguish, and to be protected
against all her enemies, she was as quickly as possible
to make herself the slave of Jesus and His most holy
Mother. She had no sooner returned to the house than
she gave herself up entirely to Jesus and His Mother
in this capacity, although up to that time she did not
so much as know what the devotion meant. Taking an
iron chain, she put it around her body and wore it until her death. After this, all her anguish and scruples
ceased, and she experienced great peace and dilation
of heart. This is what brought her to teach the devotion to many persons who made great progress in it—
among others, Father Olier, the founder of St.
Sulpice, as well as many priests and ecclesiastics of
the same seminary. One day Our Lady appeared to
her and put around her neck a chain of gold, to show
her the joy she had at Mother Agnes' having made
herself her Son's slave and her own; and St. Cecilia,
who accompanied Our Lady in that apparition, said
to the religious: "Happy are the faithful slaves of the
Queen of Heaven: for they shall enjoy true liberty."
"To serve thee is liberty."

— Seventh Motive —
It Procures Great Blessings
for our Neighbor

171. Another consideration which may bring us to
embrace this practice is the great good which our
neighbor receives from it. For by this practice we ex-

ercise charity toward him in an eminent manner, seeing that we give him by Mary's hands all that is most precious to ourselves—namely, the satisfactory and impetratory value of all our good works, without excepting the least good thought or the least little suffering. We agree that all the satisfactions we may have acquired, or may acquire up to the moment of our death, should be employed at Our Lady's will either for the conversion of sinners or for the deliverance of souls from Purgatory.

Is this not loving our neighbor perfectly? Is this not being a true disciple of Jesus Christ, who is always to be recognized by his charity? (*Jn.* 13:35). Is this not the way to convert sinners, without any fear of vanity; and to deliver souls from Purgatory, with scarcely doing anything but what we are obliged to do by our state of life?

172. To understand the excellence of this motive, we must understand also how great a good it is to convert a sinner or to deliver a soul from Purgatory. It is an infinite good, greater than creating Heaven and earth;[36] because we give to a soul the possession of God. If by this practice we deliver but one soul in our life from Purgatory, or convert but one sinner, would not that be enough to induce a truly charitable man to embrace it?

But we must remark that, inasmuch as our good works pass through the hands of Mary, they receive an augmentation of purity, and consequently of merit, and of satisfactory and impetratory value. On this account they become more capable of solacing the souls in Purgatory and of converting sinners than if they did not pass through the virginal and liberal hands of Mary. It may be little that we give by Our Lady; but, in truth, if it is given without self-will and with a disinterested charity, that little becomes very mighty to turn away the wrath of God and to draw down His mercy. It would be no wonder if, at the hour of death, it should be found that a person faithful to this practice should by means of it have delivered many souls from Purgatory and converted many sinners, though he should have done nothing more than the ordinary actions of his state of life. What joy at his judgment! What glory in his eternity!

— Eighth Motive —
IT IS AN ADMIRABLE MEANS OF PERSEVERANCE

173. Lastly, that which in some sense most persuasively draws us to this devotion to Our Lady is that it is an admirable means of persevering and being faithful in virtue. Whence comes it that the majority of the conversions of sinners are not durable? Whence comes it that we relapse so easily into sin? Whence comes it that the greater part of the just, instead of advancing from virtue to virtue and acquiring new graces, often lose the little virtue and the little grace they have? This misfortune comes, as I have shown before,[37] from the fact that man is so corrupt, so feeble and so inconstant, and yet trusts in himself, relies on his own strength and believes himself capable of safeguarding the treasure of his graces, virtues and merits.

But by this devotion, we entrust all that we possess to the Blessed Virgin, who is faithful; we take her for the universal depositary of all our goods of nature and of grace. It is in her fidelity that we trust; it is on her power that we lean; it is on her mercy and charity that we build, in order that she may preserve and augment our virtues and merits, in spite of the devil, the world and the flesh, who put forth all their efforts to take them from us. We say to her as a good child to his mother, and a faithful servant to her mistress: "Keep that which is committed to your trust. (*1 Tim.* 6:20). My good Mother and Mistress, I acknowledge that up to this time I have, through your intercession, received more graces from God than I deserve; and my sad experience teaches me that I carry this treasure in a very frail vessel, and that I am too weak and too miserable to keep it safely of myself: 'I am very young and despised' (*Ps.* 118:141); I beseech you, therefore, receive in trust all that I possess, and keep it for me by your fidelity and power. If you keep it for me, I shall lose nothing; if you hold me up, I shall not fall; if you protect me, I shall be sheltered from my enemies."

174. Listen to what St. Bernard says in order to encourage us to adopt this practice: "When Mary holds you up, you do not fall; when she protects you, you need not fear; when she leads you, you do not tire; when she is favorable to you, you arrive at the harbor of safety."[38] St. Bonaventure seems to say the same thing still more clearly. "The Blessed Virgin," he says, "is not only retained in the plenitude of the saints, but she also retains and keeps the saints in their plenitude, so that it may not diminish. She prevents their virtues from being dissipated, their merits from perishing, their graces from being lost, the devil from harming them, and even Our Lord from punishing them when they sin."[39]

175. Our Blessed Lady is the faithful Virgin who

by her fidelity to God repairs the losses which the
faithless Eve has caused by her infidelity. It is she
who obtains for those who attach themselves to her
the graces of fidelity to God and perseverance. It is
for this reason that a saint compares her to a firm
anchor which holds her servants fast and hinders them
from being shipwrecked in the agitated sea of this
world, where so many persons perish simply through
not being fastened to that anchor. "We fasten our
souls," says he, "to thy hope, as to an abiding
anchor."[40] It is to her that the saints who have saved
themselves have been the most attached and have
done their best to attach others, in order to persevere
in virtue. Happy, then, a thousand times happy, are
the Christians who are now fastened faithfully and entirely to her, as to a firm anchor! The violence of the
storms of this world will not make them founder, nor
sink their heavenly treasures! Happy those who enter
into Mary, as into the ark of Noe! The waters of the
deluge of sin, which drown so great a portion of the
world, shall do no harm to them; for "They who work
in me shall not sin," says Mary, together with the
Divine Wisdom. (*Ecclus.* 24:30). Blessed are the
faithless children of the unhappy Eve, if only they attach themselves to the faithful Mother and Virgin who
"remains always faithful and never belies herself."[41]
"She always loves those who love her" (*Prov.* 8:17)—
not only with an affective love, but with an effectual
and efficacious one, by hindering them, through a
great abundance of graces, from drawing back in the
pursuit of virtue, from falling in the road, and from
losing the grace of her Son.

176. This good Mother, out of pure charity, always
receives whatever we deposit with her—and what she

has once received as depositary, she is obliged in justice, by virtue of the contract of trusteeship, to keep safe for us; just as a person with whom I had left a thousand dollars in trust would be under the obligation of keeping them safe for me, so that if, by his negligence, they were lost, he would in justice be responsible to me for them. But the faithful Mary cannot let anything which has been entrusted to her be lost through her negligence. Heaven and earth could pass away sooner than that she could be negligent and faithless to those who trust in her.

177. Poor children of Mary, your weakness is extreme, your inconstancy is great, your inward nature is very much corrupted. You are drawn (I grant it) from the same corrupt mass as all the children of Adam and Eve. Yet do not be discouraged because of that. Console yourselves and exult in having the secret which I teach you—a secret unknown to almost all Christians, even the most devout.

Leave not your gold and silver in your coffers, which have already been broken open by the evil spirits who have robbed you. These coffers are too little, too weak, too old, to hold a treasure so precious and so great. Put not the pure and clear water of the fountain into your vessels, all spoilt and infected by sin. If the sin is there no longer, at least the odor of it is, and so the water will be spoilt. Put not your exquisite wines into your old casks, which have had bad wine in them; else even these wines will be spoilt and perhaps break the casks, and be spilled on the ground.

178. Though you, predestinate souls, understand me well enough, I will speak yet more openly. Trust not the gold of your charity, the silver of your purity, the waters of your heavenly graces, nor the wines of

your merits and virtues, to a torn sack, an old and broken coffer, a spoilt and corrupted vessel, like yourselves, else you will be stripped by the robbers—that is to say, the demons—who are seeking and watching night and day for the right time to do it; and you will infect by your own bad odor of self-love, self-confidence and self-will, every most pure thing which God has given you.

Pour, pour into the bosom and the heart of Mary all your treasures, all your graces, all your virtues. She is a spiritual vessel, she is a vessel of honor, she is a singular vessel of devotion.[42] Since God Himself has been shut up in person, with all His perfections, in that vessel, it has become altogether spiritual, and the spiritual abode of the most spiritual souls. It has become honorable and the throne of honor for the grandest princes of eternity. It has become wonderful in devotion, and a dwelling the most illustrious for sweetness, for graces and for virtues. It has become rich as a house of gold, strong as a tower of David, and pure as a tower of ivory.

179. Oh, how happy is the man who has given everything to Mary, and has entrusted himself to Mary, and lost himself in her, in everything and for everything! He belongs all to Mary, and Mary belongs all to him. He can say boldly with David: "Mary is made for me" (Cf. *Ps.* 118:56); or with the beloved disciple: "I have taken her for my own" (*Jn.* 19:27); or with Jesus Christ: "All that I have is thine, and all that thou hast is Mine." (*Jn.* 17:10).

180. If any critic who reads this shall take it into his head that I speak here exaggeratedly, and with an extravagance of devotion, alas! He does not understand me—either because he is a carnal man who has

no relish for spiritual things; or because he is a world-ling who cannot receive the Holy Ghost; or because he is proud and critical, condemning and despising whatever he does not understand himself. But the souls which are not born of blood, nor of flesh, nor of the will of man (*Jn.* 1:13), but of God and Mary, understand me and relish me—and it is for these that I also write.

181. Nevertheless, I say now, both for the former and for the latter, in returning from this digression, that the divine Mary, being the most gracious and liberal of all pure creatures, never lets herself be out-done in love and liberality. As a holy man said of her, for an egg she gives an ox; that is to say, for a little that is given to her, she gives much of what she has received from God. Hence, if a soul gives itself to her without reserve, she gives herself to that soul without reserve, if only we put our confidence in her without presumption, and on our side labor to acquire virtues and to bridle our passions.

182. Then let the faithful servants of the Blessed Virgin say boldly with St. John Damascene, "Having confidence in you, O Mother of God, I shall be saved; being under your protection, I shall fear nothing; with your help I shall give battle to my enemies and put them to flight; for devotion to you is an arm of salvation which God gives to those whom it is His will to save."

183. Of all the truths which I have been explaining with regard to our Blessed Lady and her children and servants, the Holy Ghost gives us an admirable figure in the Scriptures. (*Gen.* 27). It is in the story of Jacob, who received the blessing of his father Isaac through the skill and pains of his mother Rebecca.

This is the story as the Holy Ghost relates it. I will afterward add the explanation of it.

— Article One —
REBECCA AND JACOB

I. The Biblical Narrative

184. Esau having sold Jacob his birthright, Rebecca, the mother of the two brothers, who loved Jacob tenderly, secured this advantage of the birthright for him many years afterward by a stroke of skill most holy but most full of mystery. Isaac, feeling very old, and wishing to bless his children before he died, called his son Esau, who was his favorite, and commanded him to go out hunting and get him something to eat, in order that he might afterward bless him. Rebecca promptly informed Jacob of what had passed, and ordered him to go and take two kids from the flock. When he had given them to his mother, she prepared for Isaac what she knew he liked. She clothed Jacob in the garments of Esau, which she kept, and covered his hands and his neck with the skin of the kids, so that his father, who was blind, even though he heard Jacob's voice, might think by touching the skin of his hands that it was Esau.

Isaac, having been surprised by the voice, which he thought was Jacob's voice, made him come near. Having touched the skins with which his hands were covered, he said that the voice truly was the voice of Jacob, but that the hands were the hands of Esau.

After he had eaten, and, in kissing Jacob, had smelt the odor of his perfumed garments, he blessed him and wished for him the dew of Heaven and the fruit-

fulness of earth. He made him lord over all his
brethren, and finished his blessing with these words:
"Cursed be he that curseth thee, and let him that
blesseth thee be filled with blessings."

Isaac had hardly finished these words when Esau
entered, bringing with him what he had captured
while out hunting in order that his father might eat it,
and then bless him. The holy patriarch was surprised
with an incredible astonishment when he understood
what had happened. But, far from retracting what he
had done, on the contrary he confirmed it, for he saw
plainly that the finger of God was in the matter. Esau
then uttered great cries, as the Holy Scripture says,
and loudly accusing the deceitfulness of his brother,
he asked his father if he had but one blessing. In this
conduct of his, as the holy Fathers remark, Esau was
the image of those who are only too glad to ally God
with the world and would fain enjoy both the consolations of Heaven and the consolations of earth. At last
Isaac, touched with the cries of Esau, blessed him, but
with a blessing of the earth, subjecting him to his
brother. This made him conceive such an envenomed
hatred for Jacob that he waited only for his father's
death in order to attempt to kill him. Nor would Jacob
have escaped death if his dear mother Rebecca had
not saved him from it by her efforts and by the good
counsels which she gave him, and which he followed.

II. Interpretation

185. Before explaining this beautiful story, we
must observe that, according to the holy Fathers and
the interpreters of Scripture, Jacob is the figure of
Jesus Christ and the predestinate, and Esau that of the

reprobate. We have but to examine the actions and conduct of each to be convinced of this.

§ 1. Esau, figure of the reprobate.

(1) Esau, the elder, was strong and robust of body, adroit and skillful in drawing the bow and in taking much game in the chase.(2) He hardly ever stayed in the house; and putting no confidence in anything but his own strength and address, he worked only out of doors. (3) He took very few pains to please his mother Rebecca, and indeed did nothing for that end. (4) He was such a glutton and loved eating so much that he sold his birthright for a mess of pottage. (5) He was, like Cain, full of envy against his brother, and persecuted him beyond measure.

186. Now this is the daily conduct of the reprobate. They trust in their own strength and aptitude for temporal affairs. They are very strong, very able and very enlightened in earthly business; but very weak and very ignorant in heavenly things.

187. It is on this account that they are never at all, or at least very seldom, at their own homes—that is to say, in their own interior, which is the inward and essential house which God has given to every man, to live there, after His example; for God always dwells in Himself. The reprobate do not love retirement, nor spirituality, nor inward devotion; and they treat as little, or as bigots, or as savages, those who are interior or retired from the world, and who work more within than without.

188. The reprobate care next to nothing for devotion to our Blessed Lady, the Mother of the predestinate. It is true that they do not hate her formally. In-

deed they sometimes praise her and say they love her, and even practice some devotion in her honor. Nevertheless, they cannot bear that we should love her tenderly, because they have not the tenderness of Jacob for her. They find much to say against the practices of devotion her good children and servants faithfully perform in order to gain her affection, because they do not think that devotion necessary to salvation; and they consider that, provided that they do not hate Our Lady formally or openly despise her devotion, they do enough. Moreover, they imagine that they are already in her good graces, and that, in fine, they are her servants, inasmuch as they recite and mumble certain prayers in her honor, without tenderness for her or amendment in themselves.

189. The reprobate sell their birthright, that is to say, the pleasures of paradise. They sell it for a pottage of lentils, that is to say, for the pleasures of the earth. They laugh, they eat, they drink, they amuse themselves, they gamble, they dance, and take no more pains than Esau did to render themselves worthy of the blessing of their Father. In a word, they think only of earth and they love earth only; they speak and act only for earth and for its pleasures, selling for one moment of enjoyment, for one vain puff of honor, for a morsel of hard metal, yellow or white, their Baptismal grace, their robe of innocence and their heavenly inheritance.

190. Finally, the reprobate daily hate and persecute the predestinate, openly and secretly. They feel the predestinate are a burden to them, they despise them, they criticize them, they ridicule them, they abuse them, they rob them, they cheat them, they impoverish them, they drive them away, they bring them

low into the dust; while they themselves are making
fortunes, are taking their pleasures, getting themselves
into good positions, enriching themselves, becoming
greater and living at their ease.

§ 2. Jacob, figure of the predestinate.

(a) Conduct of Jacob

191. As to Jacob, the younger son, he was of a feeble constitution, meek and peaceful. He lived for the
most part at home, in order to gain the good graces of
his mother Rebecca, whom he loved tenderly. If he
went abroad, it was not of his own will, nor through
any confidence in his own skill, but to obey his
mother.

192. He loved and honored his mother. It was on
this account that he kept at home. He was never so
happy as when watching her. He avoided everything
which could displease her, and did everything which
he thought would please her; and this increased the
love which Rebecca already had for him.

193. He was subject in all things to his dear
mother. He obeyed her entirely in all matters—
promptly, without delaying, and lovingly, without
complaining. At the least indication of her will, the
little Jacob ran and worked; and he believed, without
questioning, everything she said to him. For example,
when she told him to fetch two kids in order that she
might prepare something for his father Isaac to eat,
Jacob did not reply that one was enough to make a
dish for a single man, but did without argument what
she told him to do.

194. He had great confidence in his dear mother.

As he did not rely in the least on his own ability, he depended exclusively on her care and protection. He appealed to her in all his necessities, and consulted her in all his doubts. For example, when he asked if, instead of a blessing, he should not receive a curse from his father, he believed her and trusted her when she said that she would take the curse upon herself.

195. Lastly, he imitated as far as he could the virtues he saw in his mother. It seems as if one of his reasons for leading such a sedentary life at home was to imitate his dear mother, who was virtuous, and kept away from bad companions who corrupt the morals. By this means he made himself worthy of receiving the double blessing of his beloved father.

(b) Conduct of the Predestinate

196. Such also is the conduct which the predestinate daily observe.

They are sedentary and homekeepers with their Mother. In other words, they love retirement and are interior. They give themselves to prayer; but it is after the example and in the company of their Mother, the holy Virgin, the whole of whose glory is within, and who during her entire life loved retirement and prayer so much. It is true that they sometimes appear without, in the world; but it is in obedience to the will of God and that of their dear Mother, to fulfill the duties of their state. However apparently important their outward works may be, they esteem still more highly those which they do within themselves, in their interior, in the company of the Blessed Virgin. For it is within that they accomplish the great work of their perfection, compared with which all their other works

are but child's play. It is on this account that, while
sometimes their brothers and sisters are working outwardly with much energy, success and skill, in the
praise and with the approbation of the world, they on
the contrary know by the light of the Holy Ghost that
there is far more glory, more good and more joy in re-
maining hidden in retreat with Jesus Christ, their
Model, in an entire and perfect subjection to their
Mother, than to do of themselves wonders of nature
and grace in the world, as so many Esaus and repro-
bates do. "Glory for God and riches for men are to be
found in the house of Mary." (Cf. *Ps.* 111:3).

Lord Jesus, how sweet are Thy tabernacles! The
sparrow has found a house to lodge in, and the
turtledove a nest for her little ones. Oh, happy is the
man who dwells in the house of Mary, where Thou
wast the first to make Thy dwelling! It is in this house
of the predestinate that he receives assistance from
Thee alone, and that he has arranged in his heart the
steps and ascents of all the virtues by which to raise
himself to perfection in this vale of tears. "How lovely
are Thy tabernacles." (*Ps.* 83:2).

197. The predestinate tenderly love and truly honor
our Blessed Lady as their good Mother and Mistress.
They love her not only in word but in truth. They
honor her not only outwardly but in the depths of
their hearts. They avoid, like Jacob, everything which
can displease her; and they practice with fervor
whatever they think will make them find favor with
her. They bring to her and give her, not two kids, as
did Jacob to Rebecca, but their body and their soul,
with all that depends on them, symbolized by the two
kids of Jacob. They bring them to her: (1) that she
may receive them as things which belong to her;

(2) that she may kill them, that is, make them die to sin and self, by stripping them of their own skin and their own self-love, so as by this means to please Jesus, her Son, who wills not to have any for His disciples and friends but those who are dead to themselves; (3) that she may prepare them for the taste of our heavenly Father, and for His greatest glory, which she knows better than any other creature; and (4) that by her care and intercession this body and soul, thoroughly purified from every stain, thoroughly dead, thoroughly stripped and prepared, may be a delicate meat, worthy of the mouth and the blessing of our heavenly Father. Is this not what the predestinate do, who by way of testifying to Jesus and Mary an effective and courageous love, relish and practice the perfect consecration to Jesus Christ by the hands of Mary which we are now teaching them?

The reprobate tell us loudly enough that they love Jesus, and that they love and honor Mary; but it is not with their substance (*Prov.* 3:9), it is not to the extent of sacrificing their body with its senses, their soul with its passions, as the predestinate do.

198. The predestinate are subject and obedient to our Blessed Lady as to their good Mother, after the example of Jesus Christ, who, of the three and thirty years He lived on earth, employed thirty to glorify God His Father by a perfect and entire subjection to His holy Mother. They obey Mary in following her counsels exactly as the little Jacob did those of Rebecca, who said to him: "My son, follow my counsels" (*Gen.* 27:8); or like the people at the marriage of Cana, to whom Our Lady said: "Whatever my Son shall say to you, that do." (*Jn.* 2:5). Jacob, for having obeyed his mother, received the blessing as it were

miraculously, although naturally he would not have had it. The people at the marriage of Cana, for having followed Our Lady's counsel, were honored with the first miracle of Our Lord, who there changed the water into wine at the prayer of His holy Mother. In like manner, all those who, to the end of time, shall receive the blessing of our heavenly Father, and shall be honored with the wonders of God, shall only receive their graces as a result of their perfect obedience to Mary. The Esaus, on the contrary, lose their blessing through their want of subjection to the Blessed Virgin.

199. The predestinate have also great confidence in the goodness and power of our Blessed Lady, their good Mother. They call incessantly for her help. They look upon her as their polar star, to lead them to a good port. They lay bare to her their troubles and their necessities with much openness of heart. They depend on her mercy and her gentleness, in order to obtain pardon of their sins through her intercession, or to taste her maternal sweetness in their troubles and weariness. They even throw themselves, hide themselves and lose themselves in an admirable manner in her loving and virginal bosom, that they may be enkindled there with the fire of pure love, that they may be cleansed there from their least stain, and fully find Jesus, who dwells there as on His most glorious throne. Oh, what happiness! "Think not," says Abbot Gueric, "that it is happier to dwell in Abraham's bosom than in Mary's; for it is in this last that Our Lord has placed His throne."[43]

The reprobate, on the contrary, put all their trust in themselves. They only eat, with the prodigal, what the swine eat. They eat earth like the toads, and, like the children of the world, they love only visible and external things. They have no relish for the sweetness of Mary's bosom. They have not that feeling of a certain resting-place and a sure confidence, which the predestinate feel in the holy Virgin, their good Mother. They are miserably attached to their outward hunger, as St. Gregory says,[44] because they do not wish to taste the sweetness which is prepared within themselves, and within Jesus and Mary.

200. Lastly, the predestinate keep the ways of our Blessed Lady, their good Mother; that is to say, they imitate her. It is on this point that they are truly happy and truly devout, and bear the infallible mark of their predestination, according to the words this good Mother speaks to them: Blessed are they who practice my virtues (*Prov.* 8:32), and with the help of divine grace walk in the footsteps of my life. During life they are happy in this world through the abundance of grace and sweetness which I impart to them from my fullness, and more abundantly to them than to others who do not imitate me so closely. They are happy in their death, which is mild and tranquil, and at which I am ordinarily present myself, that I may conduct them to the joys of eternity; for never has any one of my good servants been lost who imitated my virtues during life.

The reprobate, on the contrary, are unhappy during their life, at their death and for eternity, because they do not imitate Our Lady in her virtues, but content themselves with sometimes being enrolled in her confraternities, reciting some prayers in her honor, or going through some other exterior devotion.

O holy Virgin, my good Mother, how happy are those (I repeat it with the transports of my heart), how happy are those who, not letting themselves be seduced by a false devotion toward you, faithfully keep your ways, your counsels and your orders! But how unhappy and accursed are those who abuse your devotion, and keep not the commandments of your Son: "Cursed are all who fall from Thy commandments!" (*Ps.* 118:21).

— Article Two —
THE BLESSED VIRGIN
AND HER SLAVES OF LOVE

201. Let us now turn to look at the charitable duties which our Blessed Lady, as the best of all mothers, fulfills for the faithful servants who have given themselves to her after the manner I have described, and according to the figure of Jacob.

I. She Loves Them

She loves them: "I love those who love me." (*Prov.* 8:17). She loves them: (1) because she is their true Mother, and a mother always loves her child, the fruit of her womb; (2) out of gratitude, because they effectively love her as their good Mother; (3) because, as they are predestinate, God loves them: "Jacob I have loved, but Esau I have hated" (*Rom.* 9:13); (4) because they are entirely consecrated to her, and are her portion and her inheritance: "Let thy inheritance be in Israel." (*Ecclus.* 24:13).

202. She loves them tenderly, and more tenderly than all other mothers put together. Throw, if you can, all the natural love which all the mothers of the world have for their children into the heart of one

mother for one only child. Surely that mother will love that child immensely. Nevertheless, it is true that Mary loves her children still more tenderly than that mother would love that child of hers.

She loves them not only with affection but with efficacy. Her love for them is active and effective, like that of Rebecca for Jacob, and far beyond it. See what this good Mother, of whom Rebecca was but the type, does to obtain for her children the blessing of our heavenly Father.

203. § 1. She is on the lookout, as Rebecca was, for favorable occasions to do them good, to advance and enrich them. She sees clearly all good and evil, all prosperous and adverse fortunes, the blessings and the cursings of God; and then she so disposes things from afar that she may exempt her servants from all sorts of evils, and obtain for them all sorts of blessings; so that if there is a good fortune to make by the fidelity of a creature to any high employment, it is certain that Mary will procure that good fortune for some of her true children and servants, and will give them the grace to go through with it faithfully: "She herself takes care of our interests," says a certain saint.

204. § 2. She also gives them good counsels, as Rebecca did to Jacob: "My son, follow my counsels." (*Gen.* 27:8). Among other counsels, she inspires them to bring her the two kids, that is to say, their body and soul, and to consecrate them to her, so that she may make of them a dish agreeable to God; and she inspires them to do everything which Jesus Christ her Son has taught by His words and His examples. If it is not by herself that she gives these counsels, it is by the ministry of the angels, who have no greater honor or pleasure than to descend to earth to obey any of her

commands, and to help any of her servants.

205. § 3. When they have brought to her and consecrated to her their body and soul, and all that depends on them, without excepting anything, what does that good Mother do? Just what Rebecca did of old with the two kids Jacob brought her: (1) She kills them, makes them die to the life of the old Adam. (2) She flays and strips them of their natural skin, their natural inclinations, their self-love, their own will and all attachment to creatures. (3) She cleanses them of their spots, their vilenesses and their sins. (4) She dresses them to the taste of God, and for His greatest glory; and as it is Mary alone who knows perfectly what the divine taste is, and what the greatest glory of the Most High is, it is Mary alone who, without making any mistake, can adapt and dress our body and soul for that taste infinitely exalted, and for that glory infinitely hidden.

206. § 4. This good Mother, having received the perfect offering which we make to her of ourselves and our merits and satisfactions, by the devotion I am describing, strips us of our old garments; she cleanses us and so makes us worthy to appear before our heavenly Father. (1) She clothes us in the clean, new, precious and perfumed garments of Esau the elder— that is, of Jesus Christ her Son—which she keeps in her house, that is, which she has in her own power, inasmuch as she is the treasurer and universal dispenser of the merits and virtues of her Son, which she gives and communicates to whom she wills, when she wills, as she wills, and in such quantity as she wills; as we have seen before.[45] (2) She covers the neck and the hands of her servants with the skins of the kids she has killed; that is to say, she adorns them with the

merits and value of their own actions. She kills and mortifies, it is true, all that is impure and imperfect in them, but she neither loses nor dissipates one atom of the good which grace has done there. On the contrary, she preserves and augments it, to make it the ornament and the strength of their neck and their hands; that is to say, to fortify them and help them carry the yoke of the Lord, which is worn upon the neck, and to work great things for the glory of God and the salvation of their poor brethren. (3) She bestows a new perfume and a new grace upon their garments and adornments in communicating to them her own garments, that is, her merits and virtues, which she bequeathed to them by her testament when she died; as said a holy religious of the last century, who died in the odor of sanctity, and learnt this by revelation. Thus all her domestics, faithful servants and slaves, are doubly clad in the garments of her Son and in her own: "All her domestics are clothed in double clothing." (*Prov.* 31:21). It is on this account that they have nothing to fear from the cold of Jesus Christ, who is white as snow—a cold which the reprobate, all naked and stripped of the merits of Jesus and Mary, cannot for one moment bear.

207. § 5. Finally, she enables them to obtain the blessing of our heavenly Father, though being but the youngest born and indeed only adopted children, they have no natural right to have it. With these garments all new, most precious and of most fragrant odor, and with their body and soul well prepared and dressed, they draw near with confidence to the Father's bed of repose. He understands and distinguishes their voice, which is the voice of the sinner; He touches their hands, covered with skins; He smells the good odor of

their clothes; He eats with joy of that which Mary their Mother has dressed for Him. He recognizes in them the merits and the good odor of His Son and of His holy Mother, and so: First, He gives them His double blessing, the blessing of the "dew of Heaven" (*Gen.* 27:28), that is to say, of divine grace, which is the seed of glory: "He hath blessed us with spiritual blessings in Christ" (*Eph.* 1:3); and then the blessing "of the fat of the earth" (*Gen.* 27:28); that is to say, the good Father gives them their daily bread, and a sufficient abundance of the goods of this world. Secondly, He makes them masters of their other brethren, the reprobate. But this primacy is not always apparent in this world, which passes in an instant (*1 Cor.* 7:31), and where the reprobate are often masters. "How long shall sinners glory? Shall they utter and speak iniquity?" (*Ps.* 93:3-4). "I have seen the wicked highly exalted and lifted up." (*Ps.* 36:35). But it is nevertheless a true primacy; and it will appear manifestly in the other world for all eternity, where the just, as the Holy Ghost says, "shall reign over the nations and command them." (*Wis.* 3:8). Thirdly, His Majesty, not content with blessing them in their person and their goods, blesses also those who shall bless them and curses those who shall curse and persecute them.

II. She Fosters and Nurtures Them

208. The second charitable duty which our Blessed Lady fulfills toward her faithful servants is that she furnishes them with everything, both for their body and for their soul. She gives them double clothing, as we have just seen. She gives them to eat of the most exquisite meats of the table of God; for she gives them

to eat of the bread of life, which she herself has formed. (*Ecclus.* 24:26). My dear children, she says, under the name of Divine Wisdom, be filled with my generations; that is to say, with Jesus, the fruit of life, whom I have brought into the world for you. (*Prov.* 9:5). Come, she repeats to them in another place, eat my bread, which is Jesus, and drink the wine of His love, which I have mixed for you. (*Cant.* 5:1). As it is Mary who is the treasurer and dispenser of the gifts and graces of the Most High, she gives a good portion, and indeed the best portion, to nourish and maintain her children and her servants. They are fattened on the Living Bread, they are inebriated with the wine which brings forth virgins. (*Zach.* 9:17). They are borne at the bosom of Mary. (*Is.* 66:12). They have such facility in carrying the yoke of Jesus Christ that they feel almost nothing of its weight; the oil of devotion has made it soften and decay: "And the yoke shall putrefy in the presence of the oil." (*Is.* 10:27).

III. *She Conducts and Directs Them*

209. The third good which Our Lady does for her servants is that she conducts and directs them according to the will of her Divine Son. Rebecca guided her little Jacob, and gave him good advice from time to time; either to draw upon him the blessing of his father, or to avert from him the hatred and persecutions of his brother Esau. Mary, who is the Star of the Sea, leads all her faithful servants into a safe harbor. She shows them the paths of eternal life. She makes them avoid the dangerous places. She conducts them by her hand along the paths of justice. She steadies

them when they are about to fall; she lifts them up when they have fallen. She reproves them like a charitable mother when they fail; and sometimes she even lovingly chastises them. Can a child obedient to Mary, his foster-Mother and his enlightened guide, go astray in the paths of eternity? "If you follow her," says St. Bernard, "you cannot wander from the road." Fear not, therefore, that a true child of Mary can be deceived by the evil one, or fall into any formal heresy. There where the guidance of Mary is, neither the evil spirit with his illusions, nor the heretics with their subtleties, can ever come.[46]

IV. She Defends and Protects Them

210. The fourth good office which Our Lady renders to her children and faithful servants is to protect and defend them against their enemies. Rebecca, by her cares and artifices, delivered Jacob from all the dangers in which he found himself, and particularly from the death which his brother Esau would have inflicted on him because of the envy and hatred which he bore him; as Cain did of old to his brother Abel. Mary, the good Mother of the predestinate, hides them under the wings of her protection, as a hen hides her chickens. She speaks, she stoops down to them, she condescends to all their weaknesses. To secure them from the hawk and vulture, she puts herself round about them, and accompanies them "like an army in battle array." (*Cant*. 6:3). Shall a man who has an army of a hundred thousand soldiers around him fear his enemies? A faithful servant of Mary, surrounded by her protection and her imperial power, has still less to fear. This good Mother and powerful

Princess of the Heavens would rather dispatch battalions of millions of angels to assist one of her servants than that it should ever be said that a faithful servant of Mary, who trusted in her, had had to succumb to the malice, the number and the vehemence of his enemies.

V. She Intercedes for Them

211. Lastly, the fifth and greatest good which Mary procures for her faithful clients is to intercede for them with her Son, to appease Him by her prayers, to unite them to Him in a most intimate union, and to keep them unshaken in that union.

Rebecca made Jacob draw near to his father's bed. The good man touched him, embraced him, and even kissed him with joy, being content and satisfied with the well-dressed viands which the boy had brought him; and having smelt with much contentment the exquisite perfume of his garments, he cried out: "Behold the odor of my son, which is like the odor of a full field that the Lord hath blessed." (*Gen.* 27:27). This odor of the full field which charms the heart of the Father is nothing else than the odor of the virtues and merits of Mary, who is a field full of grace where God the Father has sown His only Son, as a grain of the wheat of the elect.

Oh, how welcome to Jesus Christ, the Father of the world to come, is a child perfumed with the good odor of Mary! (*Is.* 9:6). Oh, how promptly and how perfectly is such a child united to his Lord! But we have shown this at length already.

212. Furthermore, after Mary has heaped her favors upon her children and faithful servants, and

has obtained for them the blessing of the heavenly Father and union with Jesus Christ, she preserves them in Jesus and Jesus in them. She takes care of them, watches over them always, for fear they should lose the grace of God and fall into the snares of their enemies. "She retains the saints in their fullness,"[47] and makes them persevere to the end, as we have seen.

This is the interpretation of the story of Jacob and Esau, that great and ancient figure of predestination and reprobation, so unknown and so full of mysteries.[48]

NOTES

1. Cf. no. 110.
2. Cf. nos. 14-39.
3. Origen and St. Bonaventure, *Speculum B.V.*, lect. III, § 1, 2.
4. St. Bernard, *De Aquaeductu*, no. 6.
5. St. Bernardine of Siena, *Sermo in Nativ. B.V.*, Art. un., cap. 8.
6. St. Bernard, *Sermo III in Vigilia Nativitatis Domini*, no. 10.
7. *De Aquaeductu*, no. 18.
8. *James* 4:6. Cf. also St. Augustine, *Sermo 2 de Ascensione*, 175.
9. Cf. note on no. 113.
10. Rupert, *Prolog. in Cantic.*
11. St. Bernard, *De Aquaeductu*.
12. Cf. no. 146.
13. Cf. no. 183 and following.
14. St. Bonaventure, *Psalt. Majus B.V. Psalm* 118.
15. *"Tu es via compendiosa in caelo"* *(Laudes gloriosae Virg., S.A., VI. 939).*
16. Cf. Gradual of the Mass of the Blessed Virgin (Pentecost to Advent), and first Responsory, first Nocturn, of her Office.
17. Father Boudon was Archdeacon of Evreux and author of the book, *Le Saint Esclavage de la Mère de Dieu.*
18. The pious King Dagobert II (seventh century) consecrated himself to the Blessed Virgin as her slave (Kronenburg in *Marias Heerlijkheid*, I, 98), as also did Pope John VII (701-707). Cf. *S.A.*, X, 627.

19. Declared Doctor of the Church by Leo XII in 1828.

20. *S.A.,* X, 1310.

21. Caesarius d'Heisterbach.

22. Cf. *S.A.,* XI, 347.

23. In the year 1611.

24. The Emperor Ferdinand himself made this consecration, together with all his court, in 1640.

25. He established this devotion especially in Belgium, with Louvain, Mechlin and Brussels as principal centers.

26. Published at Anvers in 1641.

27. It was approved by the Bishops of Mechlin, Cambrai and Gand.

28. The King of Poland, Wladislaf IV, was enrolled in it at Louvain, and had the Jesuits preach it throughout his kingdom. (*S.A.,* XI, 124. ss).

29. Entitled *Mancipium Virginis,* or *The Slavery of the Virgin,* Cologne, 1634. Cf. Kronenburg, VII, 316, 317.

30. Cf. no. 159, note 17.

31. "Boudon says in his *Saint Esclavage* that the English Catholics were remarkable for this devotion in the seventeenth century." (F. W. Faber).

32. Cf. nos. 20, 21.

33. St. Germanus of Constantinople, *Sermo secunda in Dormit.* (cit. *S.A.,* VI, 37).

34. Idem, *Oratio in Encaenia venerandae aedis B.V. (S.A.,* VI, 51).

35. Office of the Blessed Virgin, first Antiphon of third Nocturn.

36. St. Augustine, *Tract 72 in Joannem,* a medio.

37. Cf. nos. 87-89.

38. *Homilia 2ª super Missus est,* no. 17.

39. *Speculum B.V.,* lect. VII, no. 6.

40. St. John Damascene, *Sermo Iª in Dormitione B.V.*

41. Application to the Blessed Virgin of St. Paul's text, *2 Tim.* 2:13.

42. Litany of the Blessed Virgin.

43. *Sermo Ia in Assumptione,* no. 4.

44. *Homilia 36, in Evangelium.* "Amamus foris miseri famem nostram."

45. Cf. nos. 25 and 141.

46. Words of St. Bernard. Cf. no. 174.

47. Words of St. Bonaventure. Cf. no. 174.

48. The preceding article (nos. 201-212) contains a beautiful exposition of the harmony existing between the childlike way of confidence in God on the one hand, and on the other, the way of filial piety toward the Blessed Virgin Mary such as is required by the holy slavery. No real opposition can be established between these different forms of devotion without danger of misunderstanding the nature of Christian life viewed as a whole. The holy slavery of love is indeed the complete expression of filial love toward our Mother Mary, whose great desire is that we be pleasing to God our Father. God is honored by the confidence we place in the Mother He has given us; trust in Mary is trust in God.

Chapter III

WONDERFUL EFFECTS
OF THIS DEVOTION

213. My dear brother, be sure that if you are faithful to the interior and exterior practices of this devotion which I will point out,[1] the following effects will take place in your soul.

— First Effect —
KNOWLEDGE AND CONTEMPT OF SELF

By the light which the Holy Ghost will give you through His dear spouse, Mary, you will understand your own evil, your corruption and your incapacity for anything good. In consequence of this knowledge, you will despise yourself. You will think of yourself only with horror. You will regard yourself as a snail that spoils everything with its slime; or a toad that poisons everything with its venom; or as a spiteful serpent seeking only to deceive. In other words, the humble Mary will communicate to you a portion of her profound humility, which will make you despise yourself—despise nobody else, but love to be despised yourself.

— Second Effect —
PARTICIPATION IN MARY'S FAITH

214. Our Blessed Lady will give you also a portion of her faith, which was the greatest of all faiths that ever were on earth, greater than the faith of all the

patriarchs, prophets, apostles and saints put together. Now that she is reigning in Heaven, she no longer exercises this faith, because she sees all things clearly in God by the light of glory. Nevertheless, with the consent of the Most High, in entering into glory she did not lose her faith. She kept it for her faithful servants in the Church Militant. The more, then, that you gain the favor of that august Princess and faithful Virgin, the more will you act by pure faith; a pure faith which will make you care hardly at all about sensible consolations and extraordinary favors; a lively faith animated by charity, which will enable you to perform all your actions from the motive of pure love; a faith firm and immovable as a rock, through which you will rest quiet and constant in the midst of storms and hurricanes; a faith active and piercing, which like a mysterious pass-key, will give you entrance into all the mysteries of Jesus, into the last ends of man, and into the Heart of God Himself; a courageous faith, which will enable you to undertake and carry out without hesitation great things for God and for the salvation of souls; lastly, a faith which will be your blazing torch, your divine life, your hidden treasure of divine wisdom and your omnipotent arm; which you will use to enlighten those who are in the darkness of the shadow of death, to inflame those who are lukewarm and who have need of the heated gold of charity, to give life to those who are dead in sin, to touch and overthrow, by your meek and powerful words, the hearts of marble and the cedars of Lebanon; and finally, to resist the devil and all the enemies of salvation.

— Third Effect —
DELIVERANCE FROM SCRUPLES, CARES AND FEARS

215. This Mother of fair love (*Ecclus.* 24:24) will take away from your heart all scruple and all disorder of servile fear. She will open and enlarge it to run the way of her Son's commandments (*Ps.* 118:32) with the holy liberty of the children of God. She will introduce into it pure love, of which she has the treasure,[2] so that you shall no longer be guided by fear, as hitherto, in your dealings with the God of charity, but by love alone. You will look on Him as your good Father, whom you will be incessantly trying to please, and with whom you will converse confidently, as a child with its tender father. If, unfortunately, you offend Him, you will at once humble yourself before Him. You will ask His pardon with great lowliness, but at the same time you will stretch your hand out to Him with simplicity, and you will raise yourself up lovingly, without trouble or disquietude, and go on your way to Him without discouragement.

— Fourth Effect —
GREAT CONFIDENCE IN GOD AND MARY

216. Our Blessed Lady will fill you with great confidence in God and in herself: (1) because you will not be approaching Jesus by yourself, but always by that good Mother; (2) because, as you have given her all your merits, graces and satisfactions to dispose of at her will, she will communicate to you her virtues and will clothe you in her merits, so that you will be able to say to God with confidence: "Behold Mary Thy

handmaid; be it done unto me according to Thy word" (*Lk.* 1:38); (3) because, as you have given yourself entirely to her, body and soul, she, who is liberal with the liberal, and more liberal even than the liberal, will in return give herself to you in a marvelous but real manner, so that you may say to her with assurance: "I am thine, holy Virgin; save me" (Cf. *Ps.* 118:94); or as I have said before,[3] with the beloved disciple: "I have taken thee, holy Mother, for my own." You may also say with St. Bonaventure: "My loving and redeeming Mistress, I will have confidence and will not fear, because you are my strength and my praise in the Lord . . . I am altogether yours, and all that I have belongs to you!"[4] And in another place: "O glorious Virgin, blessed above all created things! I will put you as a seal upon my heart, because your love is as strong as death."[5] "Lord, my heart and my eyes have no right to extol themselves, or to be proud, or to seek great and wonderful things. Yet even at that, I am not humble; but I have lifted up and encouraged my soul by confidence; I am like a child, weaned from the pleasures of earth and resting on its mother's lap; and it is on that lap that all good things come to me." (Cf. *Ps.* 130:1-2).What will still further increase your confidence in her is that you will have less confidence in yourself. You have given her in trust all you have of good about you, that she may have it and keep it; and so all the trust you once had in yourself has become an increase of confidence in her, who is your treasure. Oh, what confidence and what consolation is this for a soul who can say that the treasure of God, where He was pleased to put all He had most precious, is his own treasure also! It was a saint who said she is the treasure of the Lord.[6]

— Fifth Effect —
COMMUNICATION OF THE SOUL AND SPIRIT
OF MARY

217. The soul of our Blessed Lady will communicate itself to you, to glorify the Lord. Her spirit will enter into the place of yours, to rejoice in God her salvation, provided only that you are faithful to the practices of this devotion. "Let the soul of Mary be in each of us to glorify the Lord: let the spirit of Mary be in each of us to rejoice in God."[7] Ah! When will the happy time come, said a holy man of our own days who was all absorbed in Mary—Ah! When will the happy time come when the divine Mary will be established Mistress and Queen of all hearts, in order that she may subject them fully to the empire of her great and holy Jesus? When will souls breathe Mary as the body breathes air? When that time comes, wonderful things will happen in those lowly places where the Holy Ghost, finding His dear spouse, as it were, reproduced, in souls, shall come in with abundance, and fill them to overflowing with His gifts, and particularly with the gift of wisdom, to work miracles of grace. My dear brother, when will that happy time, that age of Mary, come, when many souls, chosen and procured from the Most High by Mary, shall lose themselves in the abyss of her interior, shall become living copies of Mary, to love and glorify Jesus? That time will not come until men shall know and practice this devotion which I am teaching. "That Thy reign may come, let the reign of Mary come."

— Sixth Effect —

TRANSFORMATION OF THE FAITHFUL SOUL
BY MARY INTO THE LIKENESS OF JESUS CHRIST

218. If Mary, who is the tree of life, is well culti-
vated in our soul by fidelity to the practices of this
devotion, she will bear her fruit in her own time, and
her fruit is none other than Jesus Christ. How many
devout souls do I see who seek Jesus Christ, some by
one way or by one practice, and others by other ways
and other practices; and oftentimes, after they have
toiled much throughout the night, they say, "We have
toiled all night, and have taken nothing!" (*Lk.* 5:5).
We may say to them: "You have labored much and
gained little";[8] Jesus is yet feeble in you. But by that
immaculate way of Mary and that divine practice
which I am teaching, we toil during the day, we toil in
a holy place, we toil but little. There is no night in
Mary, because there is no sin nor even the slightest
shade. Mary is a holy place, and the holy of holies
where saints are formed and molded.

219. Take notice, if you please, that I say the saints
are molded in Mary. There is a great difference between making a figure in relief by blows of hammer
and chisel, and making a figure by throwing it into a
mold. Statuaries and sculptors labor much to make
figures in the first manner; but to make them in the
second manner, they work little and do their work
quickly.

St. Augustine calls our Blessed Lady "the mold of
God"[9]—the mold fit to cast and mold gods. He who is
cast in this mold is presently formed and molded in
Jesus Christ, and Jesus Christ in him. At a slight ex-
pense and in a short time he will become God,*

---

*The French text shows this word in lower case, that is, *dieu*, in contrast
to the word *Dieu* ("God") at the end of the sentence. This accords with

because he has been cast in the same mold which has formed a God.

220. It seems to me that I can very aptly compare directors and devout persons, who wish to form Jesus Christ in themselves or others by practices different from this one, to sculptors who trust in their own professional skill, ingenuity or art, and so give an infinity of hammerings and chiselings to a hard stone or a piece of badly polished wood, to make an image of Jesus Christ out of it. Sometimes they do not succeed in giving anything like the natural expression of Jesus, either from having no knowledge or experience of the Person of Jesus, or from some blow awkwardly given, which has spoiled the work. But those who embrace the secret of grace which I am revealing to them I may rightly compare to founders and casters who have discovered the beautiful mold of Mary, where Jesus was naturally and divinely formed; and without trusting in their own skill, but only in the goodness of the mold, they cast themselves and lose themselves in Mary, to become the faithful portraits of Jesus Christ.

221. Oh, beautiful and true comparison! But who will comprehend it? I desire that you may, my dear brother. But remember that we cast in a mold only what is melted and liquid; that is to say, you must destroy and melt down in yourself the old Adam to become the new one in Mary.

— Seventh Effect —
THE GREATER GLORY OF GOD

222. By this practice, faithfully observed, you will give Jesus more glory in a month than by any other practice, however difficult, in many years; and I give

---

the Catholic teaching that by Sanctifying Grace one receives "a created sharing in the Divine Nature."—*Publisher*, 1999.

the following reasons for it:

§ 1. Because, doing your actions by our Blessed Lady, as this practice teaches you, you abandon your own intentions and operations, although good and known, to lose yourself, so to speak, in the intentions of the Blessed Virgin, although they are unknown. Thus you enter by participation into the sublimity of her intentions, which are so pure that she gives more glory to God by the least of her actions—for example, in twirling her distaff or pointing her needle—than St. Lawrence by his cruel martyrdom on the gridiron, or even all the saints by all their heroic actions put together. It was thus that, during her sojourn here below, she acquired such an unspeakable aggregate of graces and merits that it were easier to count the stars of the firmament, the drops of water in the sea or the grains of sand upon its shore, than her merits and graces. Thus it was that she gave more glory to God than all the angels and saints have given Him or ever will give Him. O prodigy of a Mary! Thou canst not help but do prodigies of grace in souls that wish to lose themselves altogether in thee!

223. § 2. Because the soul in this practice counts as nothing whatever it thinks or does of itself, and puts its trust and takes its pleasures only in the dispositions of Mary, when it approaches Jesus or even speaks to Him. Thus it practices humility far more than the souls who act of themselves and trust, with however imperceptible a complacency, in their own dispositions. But if the soul acts more humbly, it therefore more highly glorifies God, who is perfectly glorified only by the humble and those that are little and lowly in heart.

224. § 3. Because our Blessed Lady, being pleased,

out of great charity, to receive the present of our actions in her virginal hands, gives them an admirable beauty and splendor. Moreover, she offers them herself to Jesus Christ, and it is evident that Our Lord is thus more glorified by them than if we offered them by our own criminal hands.

225. § 4. Lastly, because you never think of Mary without Mary's thinking of God for you. You never praise or honor Mary without Mary's praising and honoring God with you. Mary is altogether relative to God; and indeed, I might well call her the relation to God. She only exists with reference to God. She is the echo of God that says nothing, repeats nothing, but God. If you say "Mary," she says "God." St. Elizabeth praised Mary, and called her blessed, because she had believed. Mary, the faithful echo of God, at once intoned: "My soul doth magnify the Lord." (*Lk*. 1:46).

That which Mary did then, she does daily now. When we praise her, love her, honor her or give anything to her, it is God who is praised, God who is loved, God who is glorified, and it is to God that we give, through Mary and in Mary.

NOTES

1. Cf. no. 226.
2. Cf. no. 169.
3. Cf. no. 179.
4. *Psalterium majus B.M.V.*, Canticum instar Isaiae 12:2.
5. *Psalterium majus B.M.V.*, Canticum instar Ex. 15.
6. *Idiota; In contemplatione B.M.V.*
7. St. Ambrose, *Expositio in Luc.*, Lib. II, no. 26.
8. *Ag.* 1:6. The exact text is: *"Seminastis multum."*
9. *Sermo 208* (inter opera Sti. Augustini): "You are worthy to be called the mold of God."

Chapter IV

PARTICULAR PRACTICES
OF THIS DEVOTION

— Article One —
EXTERIOR PRACTICES

226. Although what is essential in this devotion consists in the interior,[1] we must not fail to unite to the inward practice certain external observances. "We must do the one, yet not leave the other undone" (*Matt.* 23:23); because the outward practices, well performed, aid the inward ones; and because they remind man, who is always guided by his senses, of what he has done or ought to do; and also because they are suitable for edifying our neighbor, who sees them; these are things which inward practices cannot do. Let no worldling, then, or critic, intrude here to say that because true devotion is in the heart, we must avoid external devotion; or that devotion ought to be hidden, and that there may be vanity in showing it. I answer, with my Master, that men should see our good works, that they may glorify our Father who is in Heaven (*Matt.* 5:16); not, as St. Gregory says,[2] that we ought to perform our actions and exterior devotions to please men and get praise—that would be vanity; but that we should sometimes do them before men with the view of pleasing God, and glorifying Him thereby, without caring either for the contempt or the praise of men.

I will allude only briefly to some exterior practices, which I call "exterior" not because we do not perform them interiorly, but because they have something outward about them to distinguish them from those which are purely inward.

I. Preparatory Exercises and Consecration

227. Those who wish to enter into this particular devotion, which is not at present erected into a confraternity (though that were to be wished),[3] after having, as I said in the first part of this preparation for the reign of Jesus Christ,[4] employed twelve days at least in ridding themselves of the spirit of the world, which is contrary to the spirit of Jesus Christ, should employ three weeks in filling themselves with Jesus Christ by the holy Virgin. They can follow this order:

228. During the first week they should offer up all their prayers and pious actions to ask for a knowledge of themselves and contrition for their sins; and they should do this in a spirit of humility. For that end they can, if they choose, meditate on what I have said before of our inward corruption.[5] They can look upon themselves during the six days of this week as snails, crawling things, toads, swine, serpents and unclean animals; or they can reflect on these three considerations of St. Bernard: the vileness of our origin, the dishonors of our present state, and our ending as the food of worms. They should pray Our Lord and the Holy Ghost to enlighten them; and for that end they might use the ejaculations, "Lord, that I may see!" (*Lk.* 18:41); or "May I know myself!";[6] or "Come, Holy Ghost," together with the Litany of the Holy Ghost and the prayer which follows, as indicated in

the first part of this work. They should have recourse to the Blessed Virgin and ask her to grant them this immense grace, which must be the foundation of all the others; for this end, they should say daily the *Ave Maris Stella* and the Litany of the Blessed Virgin.

229. During the second week they should apply themselves, in all their prayers and works each day, to know the Blessed Virgin. They should ask this knowledge of the Holy Ghost; they should read and meditate on what we have said about it. For this intention they should recite, as in the first week, the Litany of the Holy Ghost and the *Ave Maris Stella,* and in addition a Rosary daily, or if not a whole Rosary, at least the beads.

230. They should apply themselves during the third week to know Jesus Christ. They can meditate upon what we have said about Him, and say the prayer of St. Augustine which they will find in the beginning of the second part of this treatise. They can, with the same saint, repeat a hundred times a day: "Lord, that I may know Thee!" or: "Lord, that I may see Who Thou art!" They should recite, as in the preceding weeks, the Litany of the Holy Ghost and the *Ave Maris Stella,* and should add daily the Litany of the Holy Name of Jesus.

231. At the end of the three weeks they should go to confession and Communion, with the intention of giving themselves to Jesus Christ in the quality of slaves of love, by the hands of Mary. After Communion, which they should try to make according to the method given further on,[7] they should recite the formula of their consecration, which they will also find further on. They ought to write it, or have it written, unless they have a printed copy of it; and they should

sign it the same day on which they have made it.

232. It would be well also that on that day they should pay some tribute to Jesus Christ and our Blessed Lady, either as a penance for their past unfaithfulness to the vows of their Baptism, or as a testimony of their dependence on the dominion of Jesus and Mary. This tribute ought to be according to the devotion and ability of each one, such as a fast, a mortification, an alms or a candle. If they had but a pin to give in homage, and gave it with a good heart, it would be enough for Jesus, who looks only at the good will.

233. Once a year at least, and on the same day, they should renew the same consecration, observing the same practices during the three weeks.

They might also, once a month or even once a day, renew all they have done, in these few words: "I am all Thine and all that I have is Thine, O most loving Jesus, through Mary, Thy most holy Mother."

II. Recitation of the Little Crown of the Blessed Virgin

234. They may recite every day of their life—without, however, making a burden of it—the Little Crown of the Blessed Virgin, composed of three Our Fathers and twelve Hail Marys, in honor of Our Lady's twelve privileges and grandeurs. This is a very ancient practice and it has its foundation in Holy Scripture. St. John saw a woman crowned with twelve stars, clothed with the sun, and with the moon under her feet (*Apoc.* 12:1); and this woman, according to the interpreters, was the most holy Virgin.[8]

235. There are many ways of saying this Crown well, but it would take too long to enter upon them.

The Holy Ghost will teach them to those who are the most faithful to this devotion. Nevertheless, to say it quite simply, we should begin by saying: "Grant that I may praise thee, holy Virgin; give me strength against thy enemies." After that, we should say the Apostles' Creed, then an Our Father with four Hail Marys and then one Glory be to the Father; then another Our Father, four Hail Marys, and Glory be to the Father, and so on with the rest; and at the end we should say the *Sub Tuum Praesidium* ("We fly to thy patronage . . .").[9]

III. The Wearing of Little Chains

236. It is a most glorious and praiseworthy thing, and very useful to those who have thus made themselves slaves of Jesus in Mary, that they should wear, as a sign of their loving slavery, little iron chains, blessed with the proper blessing.[10]

It is perfectly true that these external insignia are not essential, and a person who has embraced this devotion may very well go without them; nevertheless, I cannot refrain from warmly praising those who, after having shaken off the shameful chains of the slavery of the devil, in which Original Sin, and perhaps actual sin, had bound them, have voluntarily surrendered themselves to the glorious slavery of Jesus Christ, and glory with St. Paul in being in chains for Christ (*Eph.* 3:1; *Philem.* 9), chains a thousand times more glorious and precious, though of iron, than all the golden ornaments of emperors.

237. Once there was nothing more infamous on earth than the cross, and now that wood is the most glorious boast of Christianity. Let us say the same of

the irons of slavery. There was nothing more ignominious among the ancients; there is nothing more
shameful even now among the heathens. But among
Christians, there is nothing more illustrious than the
chains of Jesus; for they unchain us and preserve us
from the infamous fetters of sin and the devil. They
set us at liberty and chain us to Jesus and Mary; not
by compulsion and constraint, like galley-slaves, but
by charity and love, like children. "I will draw them
to Me," says God by the mouth of the prophet, "by
the chains of love." (*Osee* 11:14). These chains are as
strong as death (*Cant.* 8:6), and in a certain sense
even stronger than death in those who are faithful in
carrying these glorious chains to their death. For
though death destroys their bodies by bringing them
to corruption, it does not destroy the chains of their
slavery, which, being of iron, do not corrode so easily.
Perhaps, on the day of the resurrection of the body, at
the last judgment, these chains shall be around their
bones, and shall be a part of their glory, and be
transmuted into chains of light and splendor. Happy
then, a thousand times happy, the illustrious slaves of
Jesus who wear their chains even to the tomb!

238. The following are the reasons for wearing
these little chains:

First, to remind the Christian of the vows and
promises of his Baptism, of the perfect renewal he has
made of them by this devotion, and of the strict
obligation under which he is to be faithful to them. As
man, who shapes his course more often by the senses
than by pure faith, easily forgets his obligations
toward God unless he has some outward thing to remind him of them, these little chains serve marvelously to remind the Christian of the chains of sin

and the slavery of the devil from which Baptism has delivered him, and of the dependence on Jesus which he has vowed to Him in Baptism, and of the ratification of it which he has made by the renewal of his vows. One of the reasons why so few Christians think of their baptismal vows, and live with as much license as if they had promised no more to God than the heathen, is that they do not wear any external sign to remind them of their vows.

239. Secondly, to show that we are not ashamed of the servitude and slavery of Jesus Christ, and that we renounce the slavery of the world, of sin and of the devil.

Thirdly, to protect ourselves against the chains of sin and of the devil; for we must wear either "the chains of sinners or the chains of charity and salvation."

240. O my dear brother, let us break the chains of sin and sinners, of the world and worldliness, of the devil and his ministers; and let us cast far from us their depressing yoke. (*Ps.* 2:3). Let us put our feet, to use the terms of the Holy Ghost, into His glorious fetters and our necks into His chains. (*Ecclus.* 6:25). Let us shoulder and carry the Divine Wisdom [that is, Jesus Christ] and let us never weary of His chains. (*Ecclus.* 6:26). You will remark that the Holy Ghost, before saying these words, prepares a soul for them, lest it should reject His important counsel. See His words: "Hearken, My son, and receive a counsel of understanding and reject not My counsel." (*Ecclus.* 6:24).

241. You would wish, my very dear friend, that I should here unite myself to the Holy Ghost to give you the same counsel as His: "His chains are chains of salvation." (*Ecclus.* 6:31). As Jesus Christ on the

cross must draw all to Himself, whether they will it or not, He will draw the reprobate by the chains of their sins, that He may chain them like galley-slaves and devils to His eternal anger and revengeful justice. But He will, and particularly in these latter times, draw the predestinate by the chains of charity: "I will draw all things to Myself" (*Jn.* 12:32); "I will draw them with the bands of love." (*Osee* 11:4).

242. These loving slaves of Jesus Christ, "the chained of Christ" (*Eph.* 3:1; *Philem.* 9), can wear their chains on their feet or on their arms, around their body or around their neck. Father Vincent Caraffa, seventh Superior General of the Jesuits, who died in the odor of sanctity in the year 1643, used to wear an iron band around his feet as a mark of his servitude; and he said that his only regret was that he could not publicly drag a chain. Mother Agnes of Jesus, of whom we have spoken before,[11] used to wear an iron chain around her body. Others have worn it around their neck in penance for the pearl necklaces which they had worn in the world; while others have worn it around their arms to remind themselves, in their manual labors, that they were slaves of Jesus Christ.

IV. Special Devotion to the Mystery of the Incarnation

243. Those who undertake this holy slavery should have a special devotion to the great mystery of the Incarnation of the Word (March 25th).[12] Indeed, the Incarnation is the mystery proper of this practice, inasmuch as it is a devotion inspired by the Holy Ghost: first, to honor and imitate the ineffable dependence which God the Son was pleased to have on Mary, for

His Father's glory and our salvation—which dependence particularly appears in this mystery wherein Jesus is a captive and a slave in the bosom of the divine Mary, and depends on her for all things; secondly, to thank God for the incomparable graces He has given Mary, and particularly for having chosen her to be His most holy Mother, which choice was made in this mystery. These are the two principal ends of the slavery of Jesus in Mary.

244. Have the goodness to observe that I generally say, "the slave of Jesus in Mary," "the slavery of Jesus in Mary." I might, in good truth, as many have done before,[13] say the "slave of Mary," "the slavery of the holy Virgin"; but I think it better to say "the slave of Jesus in Mary," as Father Tronson, Superior General of the Seminary of St. Sulpice, renowned for his rare prudence and consummate piety, counseled to an ecclesiastic who consulted him on the subject. The following were the reasons:

245. First, as we are living in an age of intellectual pride, and there are all around us numbers of puffed-up scholars and conceited and critical spirits who have plenty to say against the best established and most solid practices of piety, it is better for us not to give them any needless occasion of criticism. Hence it is better for us to say, "the slavery of Jesus in Mary," and call ourselves the slaves of Jesus Christ rather than the slaves of Mary, taking the denomination of our devotion rather from its Last End, which is Jesus Christ, than from the road and the means to the end, which is Mary; though I repeat that in truth we may do either, as I have done myself. For example, a man who goes from Orleans to Tours by way of Amboise may very well say that he is going to Amboise, or that

he is going to Tours; that he is a traveler to Amboise and a traveler to Tours; with this difference, however, that Amboise is but his straight road to Tours and that Tours is only the last end and term of his journey.

246. A second reason is that the principal mystery we celebrate and honor in this devotion is the mystery of the Incarnation, wherein we can see Jesus only in Mary, and incarnate in her bosom. Hence it is more to the purpose to speak of the slavery of Jesus in Mary, and of Jesus residing and reigning in Mary, according to that beautiful prayer of so many great men: "O Jesus, living in Mary, come and live in us in Thy spirit of sanctity," etc.[14]

247. Another reason is that this manner of speaking sets forth still more the intimate union between Jesus and Mary. They are so intimately united that the one is altogether in the other. Jesus is altogether in Mary and Mary is altogether in Jesus; or rather, she exists no more, but Jesus alone is in her, and it were easier to separate the light from the sun than Mary from Jesus; so that we might call Our Lord, "Jesus of Mary," and our Blessed Lady, "Mary of Jesus."

248. Time would not permit me to stop now to explain the excellences and grandeurs of the mystery of Jesus living and reigning in Mary; in other words, of the Incarnation of the Word. I will content myself with saying these few words: We have here the first mystery of Jesus Christ—the most hidden, the most exalted and the least known. It is in this mystery that Jesus, in His Mother's womb—which is for that very reason called by the saints "the cabinet of the secrets of God"[15]—has, in concert with Mary, chosen all the elect. It is in this mystery that He has wrought all the other mysteries of His life by the acceptance which

He made of them. "When He cometh into the world, He saith: . . . Behold, I come to do Thy will, O God." (*Heb.* 10:5-9). Hence this mystery is an abridgement of all mysteries and contains the will and grace of all. Finally, this mystery is the throne of the mercy, of the liberality and of the glory of God. It is the throne of His mercy for us because, as we cannot approach Jesus but through Mary, we can see Jesus and speak to Him only by means of her. Jesus, who always hears His dear Mother, always grants His grace and mercy to poor sinners. "Let us go therefore with confidence to the throne of grace." (*Heb.* 4:16). It is the throne of His liberality toward Mary, because while the New Adam dwelt in that true terrestrial paradise, He worked so many miracles in secret that neither angels nor men can comprehend them. It is on this account that the saints call Mary the "magnificence of God"[16]—as if God were magnificent only in Mary. (*Is.* 33:21). It is the throne of His glory for His Father, because it is in Mary that Jesus Christ has calmed His Father, angered against men, and that He has made restitution of the glory which sin ravished from Him, and that, by the sacrifice He made of His own will and of Himself, He has given Him more glory than ever the sacrifices of the Old Law could give—an infinite glory, which He had never before received from man.

V. Devotion to the Hail Mary and to the Rosary

249. Those who adopt this slavery ought also to have a great devotion to saying the Hail Mary (the Angelical Salutation). Few Christians, however enlightened, know the real value, merit, excellence, and

necessity of the Hail Mary. It was necessary for the Blessed Virgin to appear several times to great and enlightened saints to show them the merit of it. She did so to St. Dominic, St. John Capistran and Blessed Alan de la Roche. They have composed entire works on the wonders and efficacy of that prayer for converting souls. They have loudly proclaimed and openly preached that, salvation having begun with the Hail Mary, the salvation of each one of us in particular is attached to that prayer. They tell us that it is that prayer which made the dry and barren earth bring forth the fruit of life; and that it is that prayer well said which makes the word of God germinate in our souls, and bring forth Jesus Christ, the Fruit of Life. They tell us that the Hail Mary is a heavenly dew for watering the earth, which is the soul, to make it bring forth its fruit in season; and that a soul which is not watered by that prayer bears no fruit, and brings forth only thorns and brambles, and is ready to be cursed. (*Heb.* 6:8).

250. Listen to what Our Lady revealed to Blessed Alan de la Roche, as he has recorded in his book on the dignity of the Rosary: "Know, my son, and make all others know, that it is a probable and proximate sign of eternal damnation to have an aversion, a lukewarmness, or a negligence in saying the Angelical Salutation, which has repaired the whole world."[17] These words are at once terrible and consoling, and we should find it hard to believe them if we had not that holy man for a guarantee, and St. Dominic before him, and many great men since. But we have also the experience of several ages; for it has always been remarked that those who wear the outward sign of reprobation, like all impious heretics and proud

worldlings, hate or despise the Hail Mary and the Rosary. Heretics still learn and say the Our Father, but not the Hail Mary nor the Rosary. They abhor it; they would rather wear a serpent than a Rosary. The proud also, although Catholics, have the same inclinations as their father Lucifer; and so have only contempt or indifference for the Hail Mary, and look at the Rosary as at a devotion which is good only for the ignorant and for those who cannot read. On the contrary, it is an equally universal experience that those who have otherwise great marks of predestination about them love and relish the Hail Mary, and delight in saying it. We always see that the more a man is for God, the more he likes that prayer. This is what Our Lady also said to Blessed Alan, after the words which I have just quoted.

251. I do not know how it is, nor why, but nevertheless I know well that it is true; nor have I any better secret of knowing whether a person is for God than to examine if he likes to say the Hail Mary and the Rosary. I say, if he likes; for it may happen that a person may be under some natural inability to say it, or even a supernatural one; yet, nevertheless, he likes it always, and always inspires the same liking in others.

252. O predestinate souls, slaves of Jesus in Mary, learn that the Hail Mary is the most beautiful of all prayers after the Our Father. It is the most perfect compliment which you can give to Mary, because it is the compliment which the Most High sent her by an archangel, in order to win her heart; and it was so powerful over her heart by the secret charms of which it is so full, that in spite of her profound humility she gave her consent to the Incarnation of the Word. It is

by this compliment also that you will infallibly win her heart, if you say it as you ought.

253. The Hail Mary well said—that is, with attention, devotion, and modesty—is, according to the saints, the enemy of the devil which puts him to flight, and the hammer which crushes him. It is the sanctification of the soul, the joy of the angels, the melody of the predestinate, the canticle of the New Testament, the pleasure of Mary, and the glory of the most Holy Trinity. The Hail Mary is a heavenly dew which fertilizes the soul. It is the chaste and loving kiss which we give to Mary. It is a vermilion rose which we present to her; a precious pearl we offer her; a chalice of divine ambrosial nectar which we proffer to her. All these are comparisons of the saints.

254. I pray you urgently, by the love I bear you in Jesus and Mary, not to content yourselves with saying the Little Crown of the Blessed Virgin, but to say five decades, or even, if you have time, fifteen decades of the Rosary every day. At the moment of your death you will bless the day and the hour in which you followed my advice. Having thus sown in the blessings of Jesus and Mary, you will reap eternal blessings in Heaven. "He who soweth in blessings, shall also reap blessings." (*2 Cor.* 9:6).

VI. Devotion to the Magnificat

255. To thank God for the graces He has given to Our Lady, those who adopt this devotion will often say the Magnificat, as Blessed Mary d'Oignies did, and many other saints. It is the only prayer, the only work, which the holy Virgin composed, or rather, which Jesus composed in her; for He spoke by her

mouth. It is the greatest sacrifice of praise which God ever received from a pure creature in the law of grace. It is, on the one hand, the most humble and grateful, and on the other hand, the most sublime and exalted, of all canticles. There are in that canticle mysteries so great and hidden that the angels do not know them. The pious and erudite Gerson employed a great part of his life in composing works upon the most difficult subjects; and yet it was only at the close of his career, and even with trembling, that he undertook to comment on the Magnificat, so as to crown all his other works. He wrote a folio volume on it, bringing forward many admirable things about that beautiful and divine canticle. Among other things, he says that Our Lady often repeated it herself, and especially for thanksgiving after Communion. The learned Benzonius [Rutilio], in explaining the Magnificat, relates many miracles wrought by virtue of it, and says that the devils tremble and fly when they hear these words: "He hath showed might in His arm; He hath scattered the proud in the conceit of their heart." (*Lk.* 1:51).

VII. Contempt of and Flight from the World

256. Those faithful servants of Mary who adopt this devotion ought always greatly to despise, to hate and to eschew the corrupted world, and to make use of those practices of contempt of the world which we have given in the first part of this treatise.[18]

— Article Two —
INTERIOR PRACTICES

257. Besides the external practices of the devotion which we have been describing so far, and which we must not omit through negligence or contempt, so far as the state and condition of each one will allow him to observe them, there are some very sanctifying interior practices for those whom the Holy Ghost calls to high perfection.

These may be expressed in four words: to do all our actions *by* Mary, *with* Mary, *in* Mary and *for* Mary; so that we may do them all the more perfectly *by* Jesus, *with* Jesus, *in* Jesus and *for* Jesus.

I. All by Mary

258. We must do all our actions *by* Mary; that is to say, we must obey her in all things, and in all things conduct ourselves by her spirit, which is the Holy Spirit of God. "Those who are led by the Spirit of God are the children of God." (*Rom.* 8:14). Those who are led by the spirit of Mary are the children of Mary, and consequently the children of God, as we have shown;[19] and among so many clients of the Blessed Virgin, none are true or faithful but those who are led by her spirit. I have said that the spirit of Mary was the Spirit of God, because she was never led by her own spirit, but always by the Spirit of God, who has rendered Himself so completely master of her that He has become her own spirit.

It is on this account that St. Ambrose says: "Let the soul of Mary be in each of us to magnify the Lord, and the spirit of Mary be in each of us to rejoice in

God."[20] A soul is happy indeed when, like the good Jesuit lay-brother, Alphonse Rodriguez, who died in the odor of sanctity,[21] it is all possessed and overruled by the spirit of Mary, a spirit meek and strong, zealous and prudent, humble and courageous, pure and fruitful.

259. In order that the soul may let itself be led by Mary's spirit, it must first of all renounce its own spirit and its own lights and wills before it does anything. For example: It should do so before prayers, before saying or hearing Mass and before communicating; because the darkness of our own spirit, and the malice of our own will and operation, if we follow them, however good they may appear to us, will be an obstacle to the spirit of Mary. Secondly, we must deliver ourselves to the spirit of Mary to be moved and influenced by it in the manner she chooses. We must put ourselves and leave ourselves in her virginal hands, like a tool in the grasp of a workman, like a lute in the hands of a skillful player. We must lose ourselves and abandon ourselves to her, like a stone one throws into the sea. This can be done simply, and in an instant, by one glance of the mind, by one little movement of the will, or even verbally, in saying, for example, "I renounce myself, I give myself to thee, my dear Mother." We may not, perhaps, feel any sensible sweetness in this act of union, but it is not on that account the less real. It is just as if we were to say with equal sincerity, though without any sensible change in ourselves, what—may it please God—we never shall say: "I give myself to the devil"; we should not the less truly belong to the devil because we did not *feel* we belonged to him. Thirdly, we must, from time to time, both during and after the action, renew

the same act of offering and of union. The more often we do so, the sooner we shall be sanctified, and attain to union with Jesus Christ, which always follows necessarily on our union with Mary, because the spirit of Mary is the spirit of Jesus.

II. All with Mary

260. We must do all our actions *with* Mary; that is to say, we must in all our actions regard Mary as an accomplished model of every virtue and perfection which the Holy Ghost has formed in a pure creature for us to imitate according to our little measure. We must therefore in every action consider how Mary has done it, or how she would have done it, had she been in our place. For that end we must examine and meditate on the great virtues which she practiced during her life, and particularly, first of all, her lively faith, by which she believed without hesitation the angel's word, and believed faithfully and constantly up to the foot of the cross; secondly, her profound humility, which made her hide herself, hold her peace, submit to everything, and put herself the last of all; and, thirdly, her altogether divine purity, which never has had, and never can have, its equal under Heaven; and so on with all of her other virtues.

Let us remember, I repeat, that Mary is the great and exclusive mold of God,[22] proper to making living images of God at small cost and in a little time; and that a soul which has found that mold, and has lost itself in it, is presently changed into Jesus Christ, whom that mold represents to the life.

III. All in Mary

261. We must do our actions *in* Mary. Thoroughly
to understand this practice, we must first know that
our Blessed Lady is the true terrestrial paradise of the
New Adam, and that the ancient paradise was but a
figure of her. There are, then, in this earthly paradise,
riches, beauties, rarities and inexplicable sweetnesses,
which Jesus Christ, the New Adam, has left there; it
was in this paradise that He took His complacence for
nine months, worked His wonders and displayed His
riches with the magnificence of a God. This most holy
place is composed only of a virginal and immaculate
earth, of which the New Adam was formed, and on
which He was nourished, without any spot or stain, by
the operation of the Holy Ghost, who dwelt there. It is
in this earthly paradise that there is the true tree of
life, which has borne Jesus Christ, the Fruit of Life,
and the tree of the knowledge of good and evil, which
has given light unto the world. There are in this divine
place trees planted by the hand of God, and watered
by His divine unction, which have borne and daily
bear fruits of a divine taste. There are flowerbeds
adorned with beautiful and varied blossoms of virtues,
diffusing odors which delight the very angels. There
are meadows green with hope, impregnable towers of
strength, and the most charming houses of confidence.
It is only the Holy Ghost who can make us know the
hidden truth of these figures of material things. There
is in this place an air of perfect purity; a fair sun,
without shadow, of the Divinity; a fair day, without
night, of the Sacred Humanity; a continual burning
furnace of love, where all the iron that is cast into it is
changed, by excessive heat, to gold. There is a river

of humility which springs from the earth, and which, dividing itself into four branches, waters all that enchanted place; and these are the four cardinal virtues.

262. The Holy Ghost, by the mouth of the Fathers, also styles the Blessed Virgin the Eastern Gate, by which the High Priest, Jesus Christ, enters the world and leaves it. (*Ezech.* 44:2-3). By it He came the first time, and by it He will come the second. The sanctuary of the Divinity, the repose of the Most Holy Trinity, the throne of God, the city of God, the altar of God, the temple of God, the world of God—all these different epithets and encomiums are most substantially true with reference to the different marvels and graces which the Most High has wrought in Mary. Oh, what riches! What glory! What pleasure! What happiness, to be able to enter into and dwell in Mary, where the Most High has set up the throne of His supreme glory!

263. But how difficult it is for sinners like ourselves to have the permission, the capacity and the light to enter into a place so high and so holy, which is guarded, not by one of the Cherubim like the old earthly paradise (*Gen.* 3:24), but by the Holy Ghost Himself, who is its absolute Master. He Himself has said of it: "My sister, My spouse, is a garden enclosed, a garden enclosed, a fountain sealed up." (*Cant.* 4:12). Mary is shut, Mary is sealed. The miserable children of Adam and Eve, driven from the earthly paradise, cannot enter into this one except by a particular grace of the Holy Ghost, which they must merit.

264. After we have obtained this illustrious grace by our fidelity, we must remain in the fair interior of

Mary with complacency, repose there in peace, lean our weight there in confidence, hide ourselves there with assurance, and lose ourselves there without reserve. Thus, in that virginal bosom, (1) the soul shall be nourished with the milk of grace and maternal mercy; (2) it shall be delivered from its troubles, fears and scruples; and (3) it shall be in safety against all its enemies—the world, the devil and sin—who never have entrance there. It is on this account that Mary says that they who work in her shall not sin (*Ecclus.* 24:30); that is to say, those who dwell in Mary in spirit shall fall into no considerable fault. Lastly, (4) the soul shall be formed in Jesus Christ and Jesus Christ in it, because her bosom is, as the holy Fathers say,[23] the chamber of the divine sacraments, where Jesus Christ and all the elect have been formed. "This man and that man is born in her."[24]

IV. All for Mary

265. Finally we must do all our actions *for* Mary. As we have given ourselves up entirely to her service, it is but just to do everything for her as servants and slaves. It is not that we take her for the last end of our services, for that is Jesus Christ alone; but we take her for our proximate end, our mysterious means and our easy way to go to Him. Like good servants and slaves, we must not remain idle, but, supported by her protection, we must undertake and achieve great things for this august sovereign. We must defend her privileges when they are disputed; we must stand up for her glory when it is attacked; we must draw all the world, if we can, to her service, and to this true and solid devotion; we must speak and cry out against

those who abuse her devotion to outrage her Son, and we must at the same time establish this veritable devotion; we must pretend to no recompense for our little services, except the honor of belonging to so sweet a Queen, and the happiness of being united through her to Jesus her Son by an indissoluble tie, in time and in eternity.

> Glory to Jesus in Mary!
> Glory to Mary in Jesus!
> Glory to God alone!

V. Manner of Practicing This Devotion When We Go to Holy Communion

§ 1. Before Holy Communion.

266. (1) You must humble yourself most profoundly before God. (2) You must renounce your corrupt interior and your dispositions, however good your self-love may make them look. (3) You must renew your consecration by saying: "I am all thine, my dear Mistress, with all that I have." (4) You must implore that good Mother to lend you her heart, that you may receive her Son there with the same dispositions as her own. You will explain to her that it touches her Son's glory to be put into a heart so sullied and so inconstant as yours, which would not fail either to lessen His glory or to destroy it. But if she will come and dwell with you, in order to receive her Son, she can do so by the dominion which she has over all hearts; and her Son will be well received by her, without stain, without danger of being outraged or unnoticed: "God is in the midst thereof, it shall not

be moved." (*Ps.* 45:6). You will tell her confidently that all you have given her of your goods is little enough to honor her; but that by Holy Communion you wish to make her the same present as the Eternal Father gave her, and that you will honor her more by that than if you gave her all the goods in the world; and finally, that Jesus, who loves her in a most special manner, still desires to take His pleasure and repose in her, even in your soul, though it be far filthier and poorer than the stable where He did not hesitate to come, simply because she was there. You will ask her for her heart, by these tender words: "I take thee for my all. Give me thy heart, O Mary."[25]

§ 2. At Holy Communion.

267. After the Our Father, just before receiving Jesus Christ, you say three times: "Lord, I am not worthy." Say the first one to the Eternal Father, telling Him you are not worthy, because of your evil thoughts and ingratitude toward so good a Father, to receive His only Son; but that He is to behold Mary, His handmaid—"Behold the handmaid of the Lord" (*Lk.* 1:38)—who acts for you and who gives you a singular confidence and hope with His Majesty: "For thou singularly hast settled me in hope." (*Ps.* 4:10).

268. You will say to the Son: "Lord, I am not worthy"; telling Him that you are not worthy to receive Him because of your idle and evil words and your infidelity to His service; but that nevertheless you pray Him to have pity on you, because you are about to bring Him into the house of His own Mother and yours, and that you will not let Him go without His coming to lodge with her: "I held Him; and I will not

let Him go, till I bring Him into my Mother's house and into the chamber of her that bore me." (*Cant.* 3:4). You will pray to Him to rise, and come to the place of His repose and into the ark of His sanctification: "Arise, Lord, into Thy resting place: Thou and the ark which Thou hast sanctified." (*Ps.* 131:8). Tell Him you put no confidence at all in your own merits, your own strength and your own preparations, as Esau did; but that you trust only in Mary, your dear Mother, as the little Jacob did in Rebecca. Tell Him that, sinner and Esau that you are, you dare to approach His sanctity, supported and adorned as you are with the virtues of His holy Mother.

269. You will say to the Holy Ghost: "Lord, I am not worthy"; telling Him that you are not worthy to receive this masterpiece of His charity, because of the lukewarmness and iniquity of your actions, and because of your resistance to His inspirations; but that all your confidence is in Mary, His faithful spouse. You will say, with St. Bernard: "She is my greatest security; she is the source of all my hope."[26] You can even pray Him to come Himself in Mary, His inseparable spouse, telling Him that her bosom is as pure and her heart as burning as ever; and that, without His descent into your soul, neither Jesus nor Mary will be formed nor worthily lodged.

§ 3. After Holy Communion.

270. After Holy Communion, inwardly recollected and holding your eyes shut, you will introduce Jesus into the heart of Mary. You will give Him to His Mother, who will receive Him lovingly, will place Him honorably, will adore Him profoundly, will love

Him perfectly, will embrace Him closely, and will render to Him, in spirit and in truth, many homages which are unknown to us in our thick darkness.

271. Or else you will keep yourself profoundly humbled in your heart, in the presence of Jesus residing in Mary. Or else you will sit like a slave at the gate of the King's palace, where He is speaking with the Queen; and while they talk to each other without need of you, you will go in spirit to Heaven and over all the earth, praying all creatures to thank, adore and love Jesus and Mary in your place: "Come, let us adore." *(Ps. 94:6).

272. Or else you will yourself ask of Jesus, in union with Mary, the coming of His kingdom on earth, through His holy Mother; or you will sue for divine wisdom, or for divine love, or for the pardon of your sins, or for some other grace; but always by Mary and in Mary; saying, while you look aside at yourself: "Lord, look not at my sins";[27] "but let Your eyes look at nothing in me but the virtues and merits of Mary."[28] And then, remembering your sins, you will add: "It is I who have committed these sins" (Cf. *Matt.* 13:28); or you will say: "Deliver me from the unjust and deceitful man" (*Ps.* 42:1); or else: "My Jesus, You must increase in my soul, and I must decrease" (*Jn.* 3:30); Mary, you must increase within me, and I must be still less than I have been. "O Jesus and Mary, increase in me, and multiply yourselves outside in others also." (Cf. *Gen.* 1:22 ff.).

273. There are an infinity of other thoughts which the Holy Ghost furnishes, and will furnish you, if you are thoroughly interior, mortified and faithful to this grand and sublime devotion which I have been teaching you. But always remember that the more you

---

*With reference to Mary, St. Louis De Montfort is obviously using the word "adore" (French *adorer*) in its secondary meaning, that is, to give homage and veneration to, rather than to denote that worship which is due to God alone. See chap. 1, §14.—*Publisher*, 1999.

allow Mary to act in your Communion, the more
Jesus will be glorified; and you will allow Mary to act
for Jesus and Jesus to act in Mary in the measure that
you humble yourself and listen to them in peace and
in silence, without troubling yourself about seeing,
tasting or feeling; for the just man lives throughout on
faith, and particularly in Holy Communion, which is
an action of faith: "My just man liveth by faith."
(*Heb.* 10:38).

NOTES

1. Cf. no. 119.

2. *Homilia 2ª in evangelium.*

3. St. Louis De Montfort's wish has been realized. The
   Archconfraternity of Mary, Queen of All Hearts, has been
   canonically erected at Rome and has many affiliated confraternities in different countries throughout the world. See page
   211.

4. These words seem to refer to some other work by St. Louis De
   Montfort which would have been used as an introduction to this
   treatise. Such might have been *L'amour de la divine Sagesse;* cf.
   chapter VII and XVI. Or, St. Louis may be referring to this
   treatise *(True Devotion to Mary).*

5. St. Bernard, Inter opera. Meditation on the knowledge of our
   human condition.

6. St. Augustine.

7. Cf. no. 266 and following.

8. For example, St. Augustine, *Tract. de Symbolo ad
   Catechumenos,* lib. IV, cap. I; St. Bernard, *Sermo super Signum
   magnum,* no. 3.

9. "We fly to thy patronage, O holy Mother of God; despise not
   our petitions in our necessities, but deliver us always from all
   dangers, O glorious and blessed Virgin."

10. It might be objected that certain decrees of the Roman Con-
    gregations have absolutely forbidden the use of little chains.
    There is nothing in these decrees concerning the private use of
    chains, especially if worn as a sign of slavery of Jesus in Mary,
    which is precisely what St. Louis De Montfort teaches. See

Analecta Juris Pontificii, First Series, col. 757. However, there is no obligation to wear such chains. The Montfort Fathers do not distribute any special chain as a sign of the Holy Slavery of Jesus in Mary. The ordinary chain which members of the Confraternity of Mary, Queen of All Hearts wear with their medal may serve—and most fittingly so—as a sign of their holy servitude to Jesus and His Blessed Mother.

11. Cf. no. 170.
12. Members of the Confraternity can gain a plenary indulgence on the feast of the Annunciation, March 25th.
13. For instance, Father Boudon, in his book referred to in no. 159.
14. Cf. page 195.
15. St. Ambrose, *De Instit. Virg.* (caput VII, no. 50).
16. Cf. no. 6, note 2.
17. *Lib. de Dignitate Rosarii,* caput II.
18. Cf. no. 227 (note 4).
19. Cf. nos. 29, 30.
20. Cf. no. 217.
21. Canonized by Leo XIII, Jan. 15, 1888. St. Alphonsus Rodriguez (1531-1617) is not to be confused with Father Alphonsus Rodriguez (d. 1616), the author of *Christian Perfection.*
22. Cf. nos. 218, 219, sqq.
23. Cf. no. 248.
24. *Ps.* 86:5. Cf. no. 32.
25. Adaptation of two texts, *Jn.* 19:27 and *Prov.* 23:26.
26. *De Aquaeductu,* no. 7.
27. Prayer before Communion, Roman Missal.
28. *Ps.* 16:2, applied to the Blessed Virgin.

— SUPPLEMENT —

Preparation for Consecration

Consecration

Little Crown

Rosary

Confraternity

PREPARATION
FOR CONSECRATION
TO JESUS
THROUGH MARY

St. Louis De Montfort advises us to prepare for the consecration by exercises which certainly are not compulsory, but which assure its great efficacy because of the purity and other dispositions which they tend to develop in our souls.

Two different periods are assigned for these exercises: a preliminary period of twelve days during which we endeavor "to free ourselves from the spirit of the world"; and a second period of three weeks: the first devoted to the knowledge of ourselves, the second to that of the Blessed Virgin and the third to that of Jesus Christ.

These periods mentioned by St. Louis De Montfort do not constitute a rigorous and unchangable division. According to circumstances, they may be lengthened or shortened. The faithful often take but three days to prepare for the annual renewal of their consecration.

The object of this consecration is to cast off the spirit of the world, which is contrary to that of Jesus Christ, in order to acquire fully the spirit of Jesus Christ through the Blessed Virgin. Hence the practices suggested by St. Louis De Montfort: renouncement of the world, knowledge of self, of the Blessed Virgin and of Jesus Christ.

First Period

— Twelve Preliminary Days —
RENOUNCEMENT OF THE WORLD

"The first part of the preparation should be employed in casting off the spirit of the world, which is contrary to that of Jesus Christ."

The spirit of the world consists essentially in the denial of the supreme dominion of God, a denial which is manifested in practice by sin and disobedience; thus it is principally opposed to the spirit of Christ, which is also that of Mary.

It manifests itself by the concupiscence of the flesh, by the concupiscence of the eyes and by the pride of life; by disobedience to God's laws and the abuse of created things. Its works are, first, sin in all its forms; and then all else by which the devil leads to sin; works which bring error and darkness to the mind, and seduction and corruption to the will. Its pomps are the splendor and the charms employed by the devil to render sin alluring in persons, places and things.

Prayers to be said every day: Veni Creator and *Ave Maris Stella.*

Reading suitable for the twelve days: Gospel according to St. Matthew, chapters 5, 6, 7.

Imitation of Christ, Book I, chapters 13, 18, 25; Book III, chapters 10, 40.

Spiritual Exercises: Examine your conscience, pray, practice renouncement, mortification, purity of heart; this purity is the indispensable condition for contemplating God in Heaven, to see Him on earth and to know Him by the light of faith.

Veni Creator

Come, O Creator Spirit blest!
And in our souls take up Thy rest;
Come with Thy grace and heavenly aid,
To fill the hearts which Thou hast made.

Great Paraclete! To Thee we cry,
O highest gift of God most high!
O font of life! O fire of love!
And sweet anointing from above.

Thou in Thy sevenfold gifts art known,
The finger of God's hand we own;
The promise of the Father, Thou!
Who dost the tongue with power endow.

Kindle our senses from above,
And make our hearts o'erflow with love;
With patience firm and virtue high
The weakness of our flesh supply.

Far from us drive the foe we dread,
And grant us Thy true peace instead;
So shall we not, with Thee for guide,
Turn from the path of life aside.

Oh, may Thy grace on us bestow
The Father and the Son to know,
And Thee, through endless times confessed,
Of both, the eternal Spirit blest.

All glory while the ages run
Be to the Father and the Son
Who rose from death; the same to Thee,
O Holy Ghost, eternally. Amen.

The Magnificat

My soul doth magnify the Lord.

And my spirit hath rejoiced in God my Saviour.

Because He hath regarded the humility of His handmaid; for behold, from henceforth all generations shall call me blessed.

Because He that is mighty hath done great things to me; and holy is His name.

And His mercy is from generation to generations, to them that fear Him.

He hath showed might in His arm; He hath scattered the proud in the conceit of their heart.

He hath put down the mighty from their seat; and hath exalted the humble.

He hath filled the hungry with good things; and the rich He hath sent empty away.

He hath received Israel His servant, being mindful of His mercy.

As He spoke to our fathers, to Abraham and to his seed forever. Amen.

Glory be to the Father, etc.

Ave Maris Stella

Hail, bright star of ocean,
   God's own Mother blest,
Ever sinless Virgin,
   Gate of heavenly rest.

Taking that sweet *Ave*
   Which from Gabriel came,
Peace confirm within us,
   Changing Eva's name.

Break the captives' fetters,
  Light on blindness pour,
All our ills expelling,
  Every bliss implore.

Show thyself a Mother;
  May the Word Divine,
Born for us thy Infant,
  Hear our prayers through thine.

Virgin all excelling,
  Mildest of the mild,
Freed from guilt, preserve us,
  Pure and undefiled.

Keep our life all spotless,
  Make our way secure,
Till we find in Jesus
  Joy forevermore.

Through the highest Heaven
  To the Almighty Three,
Father, Son and Spirit,
  One same glory be. Amen.

Second Period

— First Week —
KNOWLEDGE OF SELF

"During the first week they should employ all their prayers and pious actions in asking for a knowledge of themselves and for contrition of their sins; and they should do this in a spirit of humility." (See no 228).

During this week, we shall consider not so much the opposition that exists between the spirit of Jesus and ours, as the miserable and humiliating state to which our sins have reduced us. Moreover, the True Devotion being an easy, short, sure and perfect way to arrive at that union with Our Lord which is Christian perfection, we shall enter seriously upon this way, strongly convinced of our misery and helplessness. But how attain this without a knowledge of ourselves?

Prayers: Litany of the Holy Ghost. Ave Maris Stella. Litany of the Blessed Virgin.

Reading: Gospel according to St. Matthew, chapters 24, 25.

Gospel of St. Luke, chapters 11, 13, 16, 17, 18.

Imitation of Christ, Book I, chapter 24; Book II, chapter 5; Book III, chapters 7, 8, 13, 20, 30, 47.

True Devotion, nos. 78-82, 227, 228.

Spiritual Exercises: Prayers, examens, reflection, acts of renouncement of our own will, of contrition for our sins, of contempt of self—all performed at the feet of Mary, for it is from her we hope for light to know ourselves, and it is near her that we shall be able to measure the abyss of our miseries without despairing.

Litany of the Holy Ghost
(For private use only.)

Lord, have mercy on us.
Christ, have mercy on us.
Lord, have mercy on us.

Father all powerful, *have mercy on us.*

Jesus, Eternal Son of the Father, Redeemer of the world, *save us.*

Spirit of the Father and the Son, boundless life of both, *sanctify us.*

Holy Trinity, *hear us.*

Holy Ghost, Who proceedest from the Father and the Son, *enter our hearts.*

Holy Ghost, Who art equal to the Father and the Son, *enter our hearts.*

Promise of God the Father, *have mercy on us.*

Ray of heavenly light, *have mercy on us.*

Author of all good, *etc.*

Source of heavenly water,

Consuming fire,

Ardent charity,

Spiritual unction,

Spirit of love and truth,

Spirit of wisdom and understanding,

Spirit of counsel and fortitude,

Spirit of knowledge and piety,

Spirit of the fear of the Lord,

Spirit of grace and prayer,

Spirit of peace and meekness,

Spirit of modesty and innocence,

Holy Ghost, the Comforter,

Holy Ghost, the Sanctifier,

Holy Ghost, Who governest the Church,

Gift of God, the Most High,

Spirit Who fillest the universe,

Spirit of the adoption of the children of God,

Holy Ghost, *inspire us with horror of sin.*

Holy Ghost, *come and renew the face of the earth.*

Holy Ghost, *shed Thy light in our souls.*

Holy Ghost, *engrave Thy law in our hearts.*

Holy Ghost, *inflame us with the flame of Thy love.*

Holy Ghost, *open to us the treasures of Thy graces.*

Holy Ghost, *teach us to pray well.*

Holy Ghost, *enlighten us with Thy heavenly inspirations.*

Holy Ghost, *lead us in the way of salvation.*

Holy Ghost, *grant us the only necessary knowledge.*

Holy Ghost, *inspire in us the practice of good.*

Holy Ghost, *grant us the merits of all virtues.*

Holy Ghost, *make us persevere in justice.*

Holy Ghost, *be Thou our everlasting reward.*

Lamb of God, Who takest away the sins of the world, *Send us Thy Holy Ghost.*

Lamb of God, Who takest away the sins of the world, *Pour down into our souls the gifts of the Holy Ghost.*

Lamb of God, Who takest away the sins of the world, *Grant us the Spirit of wisdom and piety.*

V. Come, Holy Ghost! Fill the hearts of Thy faithful,

R. *And enkindle in them the fire of Thy love.*

Let Us Pray

Grant, O merciful Father, that Thy Divine Spirit may enlighten, inflame and purify us, that He may penetrate us with His heavenly dew and make us fruitful in good works, through Our Lord Jesus Christ, Thy Son, Who with Thee, in the unity of the same Spirit, liveth and reigneth forever and ever. R. *Amen.*

Litany of the Blessed Virgin Mary

Lord, have mercy on us.
Christ, have mercy on us.
Lord, have mercy on us. Christ, hear us.
Christ, graciously hear us.

God the Father of Heaven, *have mercy on us.*
God the Son, Redeemer of the world, *have mercy on us.*
God the Holy Ghost, *have mercy on us.*
Holy Trinity, One God, *have mercy on us.*

Holy Mary, *pray for us.*
Holy Mother of God, *pray for us.*
Holy Virgin of virgins, *etc.*
Mother of Christ,
Mother of divine grace,
Mother most pure,
Mother most chaste,
Mother inviolate,
Mother undefiled,
Mother most amiable,
Mother most admirable,
Mother of good counsel,
Mother of our Creator,
Mother of our Saviour,
Mother of the Church,
Virgin most prudent,
Virgin most venerable,
Virgin most renowned,
Virgin most powerful,
Virgin most merciful,
Virgin most faithful,

Mirror of justice,
Seat of wisdom,
Cause of our joy,
Spiritual vessel,
Vessel of honor,
Singular vessel of devotion,
Mystical rose,
Tower of David,
Tower of ivory,
House of gold,
Ark of the covenant,
Gate of Heaven,
Morning star,
Health of the sick,
Refuge of sinners,
Comforter of the afflicted,
Help of Christians,
Queen of angels,
Queen of patriarchs,
Queen of prophets,
Queen of Apostles,
Queen of martyrs,
Queen of confessors,
Queen of virgins,
Queen of all saints,
Queen conceived without Original Sin,
Queen assumed into Heaven,
Queen of the most holy Rosary,
Queen of peace,

Lamb of God, Who takest away the sins of the world,
   Spare us, O Lord.
Lamb of God, Who takest away the sins of the world,
   Graciously hear us, O Lord.

Lamb of God, Who takest away the sins of the world,
Have mercy on us.

V. Pray for us, O holy Mother of God,
R. *That we may be made worthy of the promises of Christ.*

Let Us Pray

Grant, we beseech Thee, O Lord God, unto us Thy servants, that we may rejoice in continual health of mind and body, and by the glorious intercession of Blessed Mary, ever virgin, may be delivered from present sadness, and enter into the joy of Thine eternal gladness. Through Christ Our Lord. R. *Amen.*

— Second Week —
KNOWLEDGE OF THE BLESSED VIRGIN

"They shall devote the second week to the knowledge of the Blessed Virgin." (See no. 229).

We must unite ourselves to Jesus through Mary— this is the characteristic of our devotion; therefore, Saint Louis De Montfort asks that the second week be employed in acquiring a knowledge of the Blessed Virgin.

Mary is our sovereign and our mediatrix, our Mother and our Mistress. Let us then endeavor to know the effects of this royalty, of this mediation, and of this maternity, as well as the grandeurs and prerogatives which are the foundation or consequences thereof. Our Mother is also a perfect mold wherein we are to be molded in order to make her intentions and dispositions ours. This we cannot achieve without studying the interior life of Mary; namely, her virtues, her sentiments, her actions, her participation in the mysteries of Christ and her union with Him.

Prayers: Litany of the Holy Ghost. Ave Maris Stella. Litany of the Blessed Virgin. St. Louis De Montfort's Prayer to Mary. Recitation of the *Rosary.*

Reading: Gospel according to St. Luke, chapters 1, 2. Gospel according to St. John, chapter 2.

True Devotion, nos. 1-48, 90-93, 105-182, 213-225.

Secret of Mary, nos. 23-34.

Spiritual Exercises: Acts of love, pious affections for the Blessed Virgin, imitation of her virtues, especially her profound humility, her lively faith, her blind obedience, her continual mental prayer, her mortification in all things, her ardent charity, her heroic patience, her angelic sweetness, her divine wisdom, and her divine purity; "these being," as St. Louis De Montfort says, "the ten principal virtues of the Blessed Virgin."

Litany of the Holy Ghost, page 180.

Ave Maris Stella, page 178.

Litany of the Blessed Virgin Mary, page 183.

St. Louis De Montfort's Prayer to Mary

Hail Mary, beloved Daughter of the Eternal Father! Hail Mary, admirable Mother of the Son! Hail Mary, faithful spouse of the Holy Ghost! Hail Mary, my dear Mother, my loving Mistress, my powerful sovereign! Hail my joy, my glory, my heart and my soul! Thou art all mine by mercy, and I am all thine by justice. But I am not yet sufficiently thine. I now give myself wholly to thee without keeping anything

back for myself or others. If thou still seest in me anything which does not belong to thee, I beseech thee to
take it and to make thyself the absolute Mistress of all
that is mine. Destroy in me all that may be displeasing
to God, root it up and bring it to nought; place and
cultivate in me everything that is pleasing to thee.

May the light of thy faith dispel the darkness of my
mind; may thy profound humility take the place of my
pride; may thy sublime contemplation check the distractions of my wandering imagination; may thy con-
tinuous sight of God fill my memory with His presence; may the burning love of thy heart inflame the
lukewarmness of mine; may thy virtues take the place
of my sins; may thy merits be my only adornment in
the sight of God and make up for all that is wanting in
me. Finally, dearly beloved Mother, grant, if it be
possible, that I may have no other spirit but thine to
know Jesus and His divine will; that I may have no
other soul but thine to praise and glorify the Lord;
that I may have no other heart but thine to love God
with a love as pure and ardent as thine. I do not ask
thee for visions, revelations, sensible devotion or
spiritual pleasures. It is thy privilege to see God
clearly; it is thy privilege to enjoy heavenly bliss; it is
thy privilege to triumph gloriously in Heaven at the
right hand of thy Son and to hold absolute sway over
angels, men and demons; it is thy privilege to dispose
of all the gifts of God, just as thou willest.

Such is, O heavenly Mary, the "best part," which
the Lord has given thee and which shall never be
taken away from thee—and this thought fills my heart
with joy. As for my part here below, I wish for no
other than that which was thine: to believe sincerely
without spiritual pleasures; to suffer joyfully without

human consolation; to die continually to myself without respite; and to work zealously and unselfishly for thee until death as the humblest of thy servants. The only grace I beg thee to obtain for me is that every day and every moment of my life I may say: Amen, so be it—to all that thou didst do while on earth; Amen, so be it—to all that thou art now doing in Heaven; Amen, so be it—to all that thou art doing in my soul, so that thou alone mayest fully glorify Jesus in me for time and eternity. Amen.

— Third Week —
KNOWLEDGE OF JESUS CHRIST

"During the third week, they shall apply themselves to the study of Jesus Christ." (See no. 230).

What is to be studied in Christ? First the Man-God, His grace and glory; then His rights to sovereign dominion over us; since, after having renounced Satan and the world, we have taken Jesus Christ for our Lord. What next shall be the object of our study? His exterior actions and also His interior life; namely, the virtues and acts of His Sacred Heart; His association with Mary in the mysteries of the Annunciation and Incarnation, during His infancy and hidden life, at the feast of Cana and on Calvary.

Prayers: Litany of the Holy Ghost. Ave Maris Stella. Litany of the Holy Name of Jesus or Litany of the Sacred Heart. St. Louis De Montfort's Prayer to Jesus. O Jesus Living in Mary.
Reading: Gospel according to St. Matthew, chapters 26, 27.

Gospel according to St. John, chapters 13 ff.

Imitation of Christ, Book II, chapters 7, 11, 12; Book III, chapters 5, 6, 56; Book IV, chapters 1, 8, 13.

True Devotion, nos. 60-67, 183, 212, 226-265.

Spiritual Exercises: Acts of love of God, thanksgiving for the blessings of Jesus, contrition and resolution.

Litany of the Holy Ghost, page 180.

Ave Maris Stella, page 178.

Litany of the Holy Name of Jesus

Lord, have mercy on us.
 Christ, have mercy on us.
Lord, have mercy on us. Jesus, hear us.
 Jesus, graciously hear us.

God the Father of Heaven, *have mercy on us.*
God the Son, Redeemer of the world, *have mercy on us.*
God the Holy Ghost, *etc.*
Holy Trinity, One God,
Jesus, Son of the living God,
Jesus, splendor of the Father,
Jesus, brightness of eternal light,
Jesus, King of glory,
Jesus, sun of justice,
Jesus, Son of the Virgin Mary,
Jesus, most amiable,
Jesus, most admirable,
Jesus, mighty God,
Jesus, Father of the world to come,
Jesus, angel of great counsel,
Jesus, most powerful,
Jesus, most patient,

Jesus, most obedient,
Jesus, meek and humble of heart,
Jesus, lover of chastity,
Jesus, lover of us,
Jesus, God of peace,
Jesus, author of life,
Jesus, model of virtues,
Jesus, lover of souls,
Jesus, our God,
Jesus, our refuge,
Jesus, Father of the poor,
Jesus, treasure of the faithful,
Jesus, Good Shepherd,
Jesus, true light,
Jesus, eternal wisdom,
Jesus, infinite goodness,
Jesus, our way and our life,
Jesus, joy of angels,
Jesus, King of patriarchs,
Jesus, master of Apostles,
Jesus, teacher of Evangelists,
Jesus, strength of martyrs,
Jesus, light of confessors,
Jesus, purity of virgins,
Jesus, crown of all saints,

Be merciful, *spare us, O Jesus.*
Be merciful, *graciously hear us, O Jesus.*

From all evil, *Jesus, deliver us.*
From all sin, *Jesus, deliver us.*
From Thy wrath, *etc.*
From the snares of the devil,
From the spirit of fornication,

From everlasting death,
From the neglect of Thine inspirations,
Through the mystery of Thy holy Incarnation,
Through Thy nativity,
Through Thine infancy,
Through Thy most divine life,
Through Thy labors,
Through Thine agony and Passion,
Through Thy cross and dereliction,
Through Thy sufferings,
Through Thy death and burial,
Through Thy Resurrection,
Through Thine Ascension,
Through Thine institution of the most Holy Eucharist,
Through Thy joys,
Through Thy glory,

Lamb of God, Who takest away the sins of the world,
Spare us, O Jesus.
Lamb of God, Who takest away the sins of the world,
Graciously hear us, O Jesus.
Lamb of God, Who takest away the sins of the world,
Have mercy on us.

Jesus, hear us,
Jesus, graciously hear us.

Let Us Pray

O Lord Jesus Christ, Who hast said: Ask and ye shall receive, seek and ye shall find, knock and it shall be opened unto you; grant, we beseech Thee, to us who ask the gift of Thy divine love, that we may ever love Thee with all our hearts, and in all our words and actions, and never cease from praising Thee.

Give us, O Lord, a perpetual fear and love of Thy holy Name; for Thou never failest to govern those whom Thou dost solidly establish in Thy love, Who livest and reignest world without end. R. *Amen.*

Litany of the Sacred Heart

Lord, have mercy on us.
  Christ, have mercy on us.
Lord, have mercy on us. Christ, hear us.
  Christ, graciously hear us.

God the Father of Heaven, *have mercy on us.*
God the Son, Redeemer of the world,
  have mercy on us.
God the Holy Ghost, *etc.*
Holy Trinity, One God,
Heart of Jesus, Son of the Eternal Father,
Heart of Jesus, formed by the Holy Ghost in the womb of the Virgin Mother,
Heart of Jesus, substantially united with the Word of God,
Heart of Jesus, of infinite majesty,
Heart of Jesus, holy temple of God,
Heart of Jesus, tabernacle of the Most High,
Heart of Jesus, house of God and gate of Heaven,
Heart of Jesus, burning furnace of charity,
Heart of Jesus, abode of justice and love,
Heart of Jesus, full of goodness and love,
Heart of Jesus, abyss of all virtues,
Heart of Jesus, most worthy of all praise,
Heart of Jesus, King and center of all hearts,
Heart of Jesus, in Whom are all the treasures of wisdom and knowledge,

Heart of Jesus, in Whom dwells all the fullness of divinity,

Heart of Jesus, in Whom the Father was well pleased,

Heart of Jesus, of Whose fullness we have all received,

Heart of Jesus, desire of the everlasting hills,

Heart of Jesus, patient and most merciful,

Heart of Jesus, enriching all who invoke Thee,

Heart of Jesus, fountain of life and holiness,

Heart of Jesus, propitiation for our sins,

Heart of Jesus, loaded down with opprobrium,

Heart of Jesus, bruised for our offenses,

Heart of Jesus, obedient unto death,

Heart of Jesus, pierced with a lance,

Heart of Jesus, source of all consolation,

Heart of Jesus, our life and resurrection,

Heart of Jesus, our peace and reconciliation,

Heart of Jesus, victim for sin,

Heart of Jesus, salvation of those who trust in Thee,

Heart of Jesus, hope of those who die in Thee,

Heart of Jesus, delight of all the saints,

Lamb of God, Who takest away the sins of the world,
Spare us, O Lord.

Lamb of God, Who takest away the sins of the world,
Graciously hear us, O Lord.

Lamb of God, Who takest away the sins of the world,
Have mercy on us.

V. Jesus, meek and humble of heart,
R. *Make our hearts like unto Thine.*

Let Us Pray

Almighty and everlasting God, graciously regard the Heart of Thy well-beloved Son and the acts of praise and satisfaction which He renders Thee on behalf of sinners; appeased by worthy homage, pardon those who implore Thy mercy, in the name of the same Jesus Christ Thy Son, Who liveth and reigneth with Thee, world without end. R. *Amen.*

St. Louis De Montfort's Prayer to Jesus

O most loving Jesus, deign to let me pour forth my gratitude before Thee, for the grace Thou hast bestowed upon me in giving me to Thy holy Mother through the devotion of Holy Bondage, that she may be my advocate in the presence of Thy majesty and my support in my extreme misery. Alas, O Lord! I am so wretched that without this dear Mother I should be certainly lost. Yes, Mary is necessary for me at Thy side and everywhere: that she may appease Thy just wrath, because I have so often offended Thee; that she may save me from the eternal punishment of Thy justice, which I deserve; that she may contemplate Thee, speak to Thee, pray to Thee, approach Thee and please Thee; that she may help me to save my soul and the souls of others; in short, Mary is necessary for me that I may always do Thy holy will and seek Thy greater glory in all things. Ah, would that I could proclaim throughout the whole world the mercy that Thou hast shown to me! Would that everyone might know I should be already damned, were it not for Mary! Would that I might offer worthy thanksgiving for so great a blessing! Mary is in me. Oh, what a treasure! Oh, what a consolation! And shall I not be entirely hers? Oh, what ingratitude! My dear Saviour, send me death rather than such a calamity, for I would rather die than live without belonging entirely to Mary. With St. John the Evangelist at the foot of the Cross, I have taken her a thousand times for my own and as many times have given myself to her; but if I have not yet done it as Thou, dear Jesus, dost wish, I now renew this offering as Thou dost desire me to renew it. And if Thou seest in my soul or my body anything that does not belong to this august princess, I pray Thee to take it and cast it far from me, for whatever in me does not belong to Mary is un- worthy of Thee.

O Holy Spirit, grant me all these graces. Plant in my soul the Tree of true Life, which is Mary; cultivate it and tend it so that it may grow and blossom and bring forth the fruit of life in abundance. O Holy Spirit, give me great devotion to Mary, Thy faithful spouse; give me great confidence in her maternal heart and an abid- ing refuge in her mercy, so that by her Thou mayest truly form in me Jesus Christ, great and mighty, unto the fullness of His perfect age. Amen.

O Jesus Living in Mary

O Jesus living in Mary,
Come and live in Thy servants,
In the spirit of Thy holiness,
In the fullness of Thy might,
In the truth of Thy virtues,
In the perfection of Thy ways,
In the communion of Thy mysteries;
Subdue every hostile power
In Thy spirit, for the glory of the Father. Amen.

THE CONSECRATION

The Day of Consecration

"At the end of the three weeks," says St. Louis De Montfort, "they shall go to confession and to Communion, with the intention of giving themselves to Jesus Christ in the quality of slaves of love, by the hands of Mary. After Communion, which they should try to make according to the method given further on [See no. 266], they should recite the formula of their consecration, which they will also find further on. They ought to write it, or have it written, unless they have a printed copy of it; and they should sign it the same day they have made it. It would be well also that on that day they should pay some tribute to Jesus Christ and our Blessed Lady, either as a penance for their past unfaithfulness to the vows of their Baptism or as a testimony of their dependence on the dominion of Jesus and Mary. This tribute ought to be according to the devotion and ability of everyone, such as a fast, a mortification, an alms or a candle. If they had but a pin to give in homage, yet gave it with good heart, it would be enough for Jesus, who looks only at one's good will. Once a year at least, on the same day, they should renew the same consecration, observing the same practices during the three weeks. They might also once a month, or even once a day, renew all they have done, in these few words: 'I am all Thine and all that I have belongs to Thee, O my sweet Jesus, through Mary, Thy holy Mother.'"

The Act of Consecration

*Consecration to Jesus Christ,
the Incarnate Wisdom,
through the Blessed Virgin Mary*

O Eternal and Incarnate Wisdom! O sweetest and most adorable Jesus! True God and true man, only Son of the Eternal Father, and of Mary, always virgin! I adore Thee profoundly in the bosom and splendors of Thy Father during eternity; and I adore Thee also in the virginal bosom of Mary, Thy most worthy Mother, in the time of Thine Incarnation.

I give Thee thanks for that Thou hast annihilated Thyself, taking the form of a slave in order to rescue me from the cruel slavery of the devil. I praise and glorify Thee for that Thou hast been pleased to submit Thyself to Mary, Thy holy Mother, in all things, in order to make me Thy faithful slave through her. But, alas! Ungrateful and faithless as I have been, I have not kept the promises which I made so solemnly to Thee in my Baptism; I have not fulfilled my obligations; I do not deserve to be called Thy child, nor yet Thy slave; and as there is nothing in me which does not merit Thine anger and Thy repulse, I dare not come by myself before Thy most holy and august Majesty. It is on this account that I have recourse to the intercession of Thy most holy Mother, whom Thou hast given me for a mediatrix with Thee. It is through her that I hope to obtain of Thee contrition, the pardon of my sins, and the acquisition and preservation of wisdom.

Hail, then, O Immaculate Mary, living tabernacle of the Divinity, where the Eternal Wisdom willed to be hidden and to be adored by angels and by men! Hail, O Queen of Heaven and earth, to whose empire everything is subject which is under God. Hail, O sure refuge of sinners, whose mercy fails no one. Hear the desires which I have of the Divine Wisdom; and for that end receive the vows and offerings which in my lowliness I present to thee.

I, (Name), a faithless sinner, renew and ratify today in thy hands the vows of my Baptism; I renounce forever Satan, his pomps and works; and I give myself entirely to Jesus Christ, the Incarnate Wisdom, to carry my cross after Him all the days of my life, and to be more faithful to Him than I have ever been before.

In the presence of all the heavenly court I choose thee this day for my Mother and Mistress. I deliver and consecrate to thee, as thy slave, my body and soul, my goods, both interior and exterior, and even the value of all my good actions, past, present and future; leaving to thee the entire and full right of disposing of me, and all that belongs to me, without exception, according to thy good pleasure, for the greater glory of God, in time and in eternity.

Receive, O benignant Virgin, this little offering of my slavery, in honor of, and in union with, that subjection which the Eternal Wisdom deigned to have to thy maternity, in homage to the power which both of you have over this poor sinner, and in thanksgiving for the privileges with which the Holy Trinity has favored thee. I declare that I wish henceforth, as thy true slave, to seek thy honor and to obey thee in all things.

O admirable Mother, present me to thy dear Son as His eternal slave, so that as He has redeemed me by thee, by thee He may receive me! O Mother of mercy, grant me the grace to obtain the true Wisdom of God; and for that end receive me among those whom thou lovest and teachest, whom thou leadest, nourishest and protectest as thy children and thy slaves.

O faithful Virgin, make me in all things so perfect a disciple, imitator and slave of the Incarnate Wisdom, Jesus Christ thy Son, that I may attain, by thine intercession and by thine example, to the fullness of His age on earth and of His glory in Heaven. Amen.

THE LITTLE CROWN
OF THE
BLESSED VIRGIN MARY

St. John the Evangelist saw a woman crowned with twelve stars, clothed with the sun, and the moon under her feet. According to the commentators, this woman is the Blessed Virgin Mary, with her virtues and her privileges, expecially that of her divine maternity. Thus originated the *Little Crown of the Twelve Stars of the Blessed Virgin Mary,* which St. Joseph Calasanctius, St. John Berchmans and many other saints made it a practice to recite frequently.

In order to make this prayer more attractive, St. Louis De Montfort added to each *Hail Mary* one of the praises of the Blessed Virgin, with the invocation, "Rejoice, O Virgin Mary; rejoice a thousand times."

It is this prayer which St. Louis De Montfort gave to his religious families (The Montfort Fathers and the Daughters of Wisdom) as their morning prayer. He also recommends it to all those who embrace the devotion of the holy and loving slavery of Jesus through Mary.

Little Crown of the Blessed Virgin Mary

I. Crown of Excellence

(To honor the divine maternity of the Blessed Virgin, her ineffable virginity, her purity without stain and her innumerable virtues.)

1. *Our Father. Hail Mary.*

Blessed art thou, O Virgin Mary, who didst bear the Lord, the Creator of the world; thou didst give birth to Him Who made thee, and remainest a virgin forever.

Rejoice, O Virgin Mary; rejoice a thousand times!

2. *Hail Mary.*

O holy and immaculate Virgin, I know not with what praise to extoll thee, since thou didst bear in thy womb the very One Whom the heavens cannot contain.

Rejoice, O Virgin Mary; rejoice a thousand times!

3. *Hail Mary.*

Thou art all fair, O Virgin Mary, and there is no stain in thee.

Rejoice, O Virgin Mary; rejoice a thousand times!

4. *Hail Mary.*

Thy virtues, O Virgin, surpass the stars in number.

Rejoice, O Virgin Mary; rejoice a thousand times!

Glory be to the Father.

II. Crown of Power

(To honor the royalty of the Blessed Virgin, her magnificence, her universal mediation and the strength of her rule.)

5. *Our Father. Hail Mary.*

Glory be to thee, O Empress of the world! Bring us with thee to the joys of Heaven.

Rejoice, O Virgin Mary; rejoice a thousand times!

6. *Hail Mary.*

Glory be to thee, O treasure house of the Lord's graces! Grant us a share in thy riches.

Rejoice, O Virgin Mary; rejoice a thousand times!

7. *Hail Mary.*

Glory be to thee, O Mediatrix between God and man! Through thee may the Almighty be favorable to us.

Rejoice, O Virgin Mary; rejoice a thousand times!

8. *Hail Mary.*

Glory be to thee who destroyest heresies and crushest demons! Be thou our loving guide.

Rejoice, O Virgin Mary; rejoice a thousand times!

Glory be to the Father.

III. Crown of Goodness

(To honor the mercy of the Blessed Virgin toward sinners, the poor, the just and the dying.)

9. *Our Father. Hail Mary.*

Glory be to thee, O refuge of sinners! Intercede for us with God.

Rejoice, O Virgin Mary; rejoice a thousand times!

10. *Hail Mary.*

Glory be to thee, O Mother of orphans! Render the Almighty favorable to us.

Rejoice, O Virgin Mary; rejoice a thousand times!

11. *Hail Mary.*

Glory be to thee, O joy of the just! Lead us with thee to the joys of Heaven.

Rejoice, O Virgin Mary; rejoice a thousand times!

12. *Hail Mary.*

Glory be to thee who art ever ready to assist us in life and in death! Lead us with thee to the kingdom of Heaven!

Rejoice, O Virgin Mary; rejoice a thousand times!

Glory be to the Father.

Let Us Pray

Hail, Mary, Daughter of God the Father; Hail, Mary, Mother of God the Son; Hail, Mary, Spouse of the Holy Ghost; Hail, Mary, Temple of the most Holy Trinity; Hail, Mary, my Mistress, my treasure, my joy, Queen of my heart; my Mother, my life, my sweetness, my dearest hope—yea, my heart and my soul! I am all thine and all that I have is Thine, O Virgin blessed above all things! Let thy soul be in me to magnify the Lord; let thy spirit be in me to rejoice in God. Set thyself, O faithful Virgin, as a seal upon my heart, that in thee and through thee I may be found faithful to God. Receive me, O gracious Virgin, among those whom thou lovest and teachest, whom thou leadest, nourishest and protectest as thy children. Grant that for love of thee I may despise all earthly consolations and ever cling to those of Heaven until, through the Holy Ghost, thy faithful Spouse, and through thee, His faithful spouse, Jesus Christ thy Son be formed in me for the glory of the Father. Amen.

THE HOLY ROSARY
ACCORDING TO
THE METHOD OF
ST. LOUIS DE MONTFORT

Introductory Prayer

I unite with all the saints in Heaven, with all the just on earth and with all the faithful here present. I unite with Thee, O my Jesus, in order to praise worthily Thy holy Mother and to praise Thee in her and through her. I renounce all the distractions I may have during this Rosary, which I wish to say with modesty, attention and devotion, just as if it were to be the last of my life.

We offer Thee, O most Holy Trinity, this *Creed* in honor of all the mysteries of our Faith; this *Our Father* and these three *Hail Marys* in honor of the unity of Thy Essence and the Trinity of Thy Persons. We ask of Thee a lively faith, a firm hope and an ardent charity. Amen.

Apostles' Creed, Our Father, 3 Hail Marys, Glory Be.

The Five Joyful Mysteries

1. *The Annunciation*

We offer Thee, O Lord Jesus, this first decade in honor of Thine Incarnation in Mary's womb, and we ask of Thee, through this Mystery and through her intercession, a profound humility. Amen.

Our Father, 10 Hail Marys, Glory Be to the Father. O my Jesus, forgive us our sins, save us from the fires of Hell; lead all souls to Heaven, especially those in most need of Thy mercy. (Prayer to be said at the end of each decade in accord with Our Lady of Fatima's requests in 1917).

May the grace of the Mystery of the Annunciation come down into our souls. Amen.

2. *The Visitation*

We offer Thee, O Lord Jesus, this second decade in honor of the Visitation of Thy holy Mother to her cousin St. Elizabeth and the sanctification of St. John the Baptist, and we ask of Thee, through this Mystery and through the intercession of Thy holy Mother, charity toward our neighbor. Amen.

Our Father, 10 Hail Marys, Glory Be to the Father, O my Jesus.

May the grace of the Mystery of the Visitation come down into our souls. Amen.

3. *The Nativity*

We offer Thee, O Lord Jesus, this third decade in honor of Thy Nativity in the stable of Bethlehem, and we ask of Thee, through this Mystery and through the intercession of Thy holy Mother, detachment from the things of the world, contempt of riches and love of poverty. Amen.

Our Father, 10 Hail Marys, Glory Be to the Father, O my Jesus.

May the grace of the Mystery of the Nativity come down into our souls. Amen.

4. *The Presentation in the Temple*

We offer Thee, O Lord Jesus, this fourth decade in honor of Thy Presentation in the Temple and the Purification of Mary, and we ask of Thee, through this Mystery and through the intercession of Thy holy Mother, purity of body and soul. Amen.

Our Father, 10 Hail Marys, Glory Be to the Father, O my Jesus.

May the grace of the Mystery of the Presentation in the Temple come down into our souls. Amen.

5. *The Finding of Our Lord in the Temple*

We offer Thee, O Lord Jesus, this fifth decade in honor of Mary's finding Thee in the Temple, and we ask of Thee, through this Mystery and through her intercession, the gift of true wisdom. Amen.

Our Father, 10 Hail Marys, Glory Be to the Father, O my Jesus.

May the grace of the Mystery of the Finding of Our Lord in the Temple come down into our souls. Amen.

The Five Sorrowful Mysteries

1. *The Agony in the Garden*

We offer Thee, O Lord Jesus, this sixth decade in honor of Thine Agony in the Garden of Olives, and we ask of Thee, through this Mystery and through the intercession of Thy holy Mother, contrition for our sins. Amen.

Our Father, 10 Hail Marys, Glory Be to the Father, O my Jesus.

May the grace of the Mystery of the Agony in the Garden come down into our souls. Amen.

2. *The Scourging*

We offer Thee, O Lord Jesus, this seventh decade in honor of Thy bloody Scourging, and we ask of Thee, through this Mystery and through the intercession of Thy holy Mother, the grace of mortifying our senses. Amen.

Our Father, 10 Hail Marys, Glory Be to the Father, O my Jesus.

May the grace of the Mystery of the Scourging come down into our souls. Amen.

3. *The Crowning with Thorns*

We offer Thee, O Lord Jesus, this eighth decade in honor of Thy being crowned with thorns, and we ask of Thee, through this Mystery and through the intercession of Thy holy Mother, contempt of the world. Amen.

Our Father, 10 Hail Marys, Glory Be to the Father, O my Jesus.

May the grace of the Mystery of the Crowning with Thorns come down into our souls. Amen.

4. *The Carrying of the Cross*

We offer Thee, O Lord Jesus, this ninth decade in honor of Thy carrying of the Cross, and we ask of Thee, through this Mystery and through the intercession of Thy holy Mother, patience in bearing our crosses. Amen.

Our Father, 10 Hail Marys, Glory Be to the Father, O my Jesus.

May the grace of the Mystery of the Carrying of the Cross come down into our souls. Amen.

5. *The Crucifixion*

We offer Thee, O Lord Jesus, this tenth decade in honor of Thy Crucifixion and ignominious death on Calvary and we ask of Thee, through this Mystery and through the intercession of Thy holy Mother, the conversion of sinners, the perseverance of the just and the relief of the souls in Purgatory. Amen.

Our Father, 10 Hail Marys, Glory Be to the Father, O my Jesus.

May the grace of the Mystery of the Crucifixion come down into our souls. Amen.

The Five Glorious Mysteries

1. *The Resurrection*

We offer Thee, O Lord Jesus, this eleventh decade in honor of Thy glorious Resurrection, and we ask of Thee, through this Mystery and through the intercession of Thy holy Mother, love of God and fervor in Thy service. Amen.

Our Father, 10 Hail Marys, Glory Be to the Father, O my Jesus.

May the grace of the Mystery of the Resurrection come down into our souls. Amen.

2. *The Ascension*

We offer Thee, O Lord Jesus, this twelfth decade in honor of Thy triumphant Ascension, and we ask of Thee, through this Mystery and through the intercession of Thy holy Mother, an ardent desire for Heaven, our true home. Amen.

Our Father, 10 Hail Marys, Glory Be to the Father, O my Jesus.

May the grace of the Mystery of the Ascension come down into our souls. Amen.

3. *The Descent of the Holy Ghost*

We offer Thee, O Lord Jesus, this thirteenth decade in honor of the Mystery of Pentecost, and we ask of Thee, through this Mystery and through the intercession of Thy holy Mother, the coming of the Holy Ghost into our souls. Amen.

Our Father, 10 Hail Marys, Glory Be to the Father, O my Jesus.

May the grace of the Mystery of Pentecost come down into our souls. Amen.

4. *The Assumption*

We offer Thee, O Lord Jesus, this fourteenth decade in honor of the resurrection and triumphant Assumption of Thy holy Mother into Heaven, and we ask of Thee, through this Mystery and through her intercession, a tender devotion for so good a Mother. Amen.

Our Father, 10 Hail Marys, Glory Be to the Father, O my Jesus.

May the grace of the Mystery of the Assumption come down into our souls. Amen.

5. *The Coronation of the Blessed Virgin*

We offer Thee, O Lord Jesus, this fifteenth decade in honor of the Coronation of Thy holy Mother, and we ask of Thee, through this Mystery and through her intercession, perseverance in grace and a crown of glory hereafter. Amen.

Our Father, 10 Hail Marys, Glory Be to the Father, O my Jesus.

May the grace of the Mystery of the Coronation of the Blessed Virgin come down into our souls. Amen.

Concluding Prayer

Hail Mary, beloved Daughter of the Eternal Father, admirable Mother of the Son, faithful Spouse of the Holy Ghost, august Temple of the most Holy Trinity! Hail, sovereign princess, to whom all owe subjection in Heaven and on earth! Hail, sure refuge of sinners, Our Lady of Mercy, who hast never refused any request. All sinful though I am, I cast myself at thy feet and beseech thee to obtain from Jesus, thy beloved Son, contrition and pardon for all my sins, as well as the gift of divine wisdom. I consecrate myself entirely to thee with all that I have. I choose thee today for my Mother and Mistress. Treat me, then, as the least of thy children and the most obedient of thy servants. Listen, my princess, listen to the sighs of a heart that desires to love and serve thee faithfully. Let it never be said that of all those who have had recourse to thee, I was the first to be abandoned. O my hope, O my life, O my faithful and Immaculate Virgin Mary, defend me, nourish me, hear me, teach me and save me. Amen.

THE CONFRATERNITY OF MARY, QUEEN OF ALL HEARTS

It is recommended that persons making the consecration register as members of the Confraternity of Mary, Queen of All Hearts.

It is not necessary to join any religious group in order to make and live St. Louis De Montfort's consecration to Jesus through Mary. However, those who so desire may join the Confraternity of Mary, Queen of All Hearts (a religious group which the Church classifies as a "pious union" of the faithful).

The Confraternity of Mary, Queen of All Hearts was first established in Canada, by Archbishop Duhamel of Ottawa, on March 25, 1899. On April 28, 1913, Pope St. Pius X erected it as an Archconfraternity in Rome. Today there are branches of the Confraternity in various parts of the world: the United States, Canada, Haiti, South America, Europe, Asia and Africa. There are several hundred thousand members throughout the world.

Purpose

The purpose of the Confraternity of Mary, Queen of All Hearts is to help the members live and publicize the Marian way of life as the easier and more secure means to sanctify themselves. This Marian way of life is explained in the writings of St. Louis De Montfort; its object is to establish within us the reign of Mary as a means of establishing more perfectly the reign of Jesus in our souls.

In keeping with the specific purpose determined in its Constitutions as approved by the Holy See, the Company of Mary employs this Confraternity as an aid to restore the reign of Christ through Mary. The prescribed means to fulfill this purpose is the zealous promotion of the Consecration to Mary, Queen of All Hearts.

Admission

Any Catholic, including clerics and religious, may become a member of the Confraternity of Mary, Queen of All Hearts.

In accordance with the General Moderator's directives, the members may assume other obligations special to their spiritual life or their apostolate.

Membership in the Confraternity is acquired by entering the applicant's name in the official register. This is done by sending in one's name to the Father Director of the Montfort Fathers (see page 215) to be recorded in the official register; the Father Director will then send the new member a membership certificate.

Prior to enrollment, the applicant must consecrate himself to the Blessed Virgin (preferably on one of her feast days), using for this purpose the consecration of St. Louis De Montfort. (See page 197).

Obligations

In keeping with the purpose of the Confraternity, the members apply themselves zealously to live always in dependence on Mary and to perform all their actions in union with her—doing all things with Mary, through Mary, in Mary, and for Mary. By this means, they will more perfectly live and act with, through, in, and for Jesus Christ.

Thus they should renew their consecration faithfully and frequently, making a special practice of renewing it every morning at the beginning of each new day. Their donation of themselves can easily be renewed from time to time during the day by repeating the short formula: "I am all Thine and all I have is Thine, O most loving Jesus, through Mary, Thy holy Mother." The consecration can even be renewed by a mere interior act of the mind.

The members also have an obligation to publicize Marian teaching, especially that of St. Louis De Montfort, that all may come to acknowledge and honor the Blessed Virgin as their Mother and Queen.

Recommended Practices

It is commendable to make a small offering or to do a good work in honor of Our Lady on the day of Consecration. "It would be well," says St. Louis De Montfort, "that on that day they should pay some tribute to Jesus Christ and our Blessed Lady. . . . This tribute ought to be according to the devotion and ability of each one, such as a fast, a mortification, an alms or a candle."

It is also recommended to wear the medal of Mary, Queen of All Hearts.

Share in Good Works

The members share in all the good works and

prayers of the members of the Company of Mary and the Daughters of Wisdom.

The Masses offered by the members of the Company of Mary (Montfort Fathers) on the first Monday of every month for the deceased of their Congregation are applied also to the deceased members of the Confraternity.

Feasts of the Confraternity

The Annunciation (March 25) is the principal feast of the Confraternity. On this feast, there is recalled to our minds the great truth of Our Divine Lord's Incarnation and that He came to us through Mary and willed to submit Himself to her, His holy Mother.

The feast of St. Louis De Montfort (April 28) is the second principal feast of the Confraternity.

Other special feasts of the Confraternity are the Immaculate Conception (December 8), Christmas (December 25), the Purification (February 2), the Visitation (July 2), the Assumption (August 15), the Immaculate Heart of Mary (August 22), the feast of Our Lady of Sorrows (September 15).

Indulgences

The members of the Confraternity may gain a plenary indulgence, under the usual conditions, on the day of their enrollment as well as for renewing their consecration on the anniversary of enrollment, on the universal feasts of Our Lord and the Blessed Virgin, on the feast of St. Louis De Montfort, and on the first Saturday of every month. (Sacred Penitentiary, July 2, 1956).

The "usual conditions" consist of Confession, Holy Communion, prayers for the intention of the Holy Father—for example, an *Our Father* and a *Hail Mary*—and being free from all attachment to sin, even venial sin.

They may also gain a plenary indulgence at the moment of death on condition that, having received the Sacraments of Penance and Holy Communion or, if this be impossible, being of contrite heart, they invoke the Sacred Name of Jesus verbally or mentally and patiently accept death as a punishment of and as coming from the hand of God.

The members may gain a partial indulgence each time they say with a contrite heart the invocation: "I am all Thine and all I have I give to Thee, my loving Jesus, through Mary, Thy most holy Mother."

They may also gain a partial indulgence each time they perform a work of piety or charity with a contrite heart and in the spirit of the Confraternity. (Holy Office, December 18, 1913).

For further information, one should write to:

Reverend Father Director
The Confraternity
Montfort Fathers
26 South Saxon Ave.
Bay Shore, N.Y. 11706

***If you have enjoyed this book, consider making your next
selection from among the following . . .***

Visits to the Blessed Sacrament. *St. Alphonsus.* 5.00
Glories of Divine Grace. *Scheeben.* 18.00
Angels & Devils. *Joan Carroll Cruz* 15.00
Creation Rediscovered. *Keane* 21.00
Spiritual Exercises of St. Ignatius 12.50
Catholic Controversy. *St. Francis de Sales* 15.00
Eucharistic Miracles. *Joan Carroll Cruz* 15.00
The Incorruptibles. *Joan Carroll Cruz* 13.50
Padre Pio—The Stigmatist. *Fr. Charles Carty* 15.00
Secret of Mary. *St. Louis De Montfort* 5.00
Ven. Francisco Marto of Fatima. *Cirrincione,* comp. 1.50
Little Catechism of the Curé of Ars. *St. John Vianney* 6.00
The Curé of Ars—Patron St. of Parish Priests. *O'Brien* 5.50
The Four Last Things: Death, Judgment, Hell, Heaven 7.00
Pope St. Pius X. *F. A. Forbes* 8.00
Confession of a Roman Catholic. *Paul Whitcomb* 1.50
The Catholic Church Has the Answer. *Paul Whitcomb* 1.50
The Sinner's Guide. *Ven. Louis of Granada* 12.00
True Devotion to Mary. *St. Louis De Montfort* 8.00
I Wait for You. *Sr. Josefa Menendez* 75
Words of Love. *Menendez, Betrone, Mary of the Trinity.* 6.00
Prayer—The Key to Salvation. *Fr. Michael Müller* 7.50
Sermons of St. Alphonsus Liguori for Every Sunday 16.50
A Catechism of Modernism. *Fr. J. B. Lemius* 5.00
Life of Blessed Margaret of Castello. *Fr. Bonniwell* 7.50
The Ways of Mental Prayer. *Dom Vitalis Lehodey* 14.00
The Story of the Church. *Johnson, Hannan, Dominica* 16.50
Hell Quizzes. *Radio Replies Press* 1.50
Purgatory Quizzes. *Radio Replies Press* 1.50
Eucharist Quizzes. *Radio Replies Press* 1.50
Meditation Prayer on Mary Immaculate. *Padre Pio* 1.50
Textual Concordance of/Holy Scriptures. *Williams.* PB 35.00
The Way of Divine Love. (pocket, unabr.). *Menendez* 8.50
Mystical City of God—Abridged. *Ven. Mary of Agreda* 18.50

***At your Bookdealer or direct from the Publisher.
Call Toll Free 1-800-437-5876.***

Prices subject to change.